About the Author

DAVID OVASON teaches astrology, and has studied the life and writings of Nostradamus for more than forty years. He is the author of several books, including *The Secret Architecture of Our Nation's Capital*, and he lives and works in England.

Also by David Ovason

Nostradamus: Prophecies for America

The Secret Architecture of Our Nation's Capital:
The Masons and the Building of Washington, D.C.

The Secrets of Nostradamus:
A Radical New Interpretation of the Master's Prophecies

The
SECRET
SYMBOLS
of the
DOLLAR
BILL

A Closer Look at the Hidden Magic and Meaning of the Money You Use Everyday

DAVID OVASON

 Perennial Currents

An Imprint of HarperCollinsPublishers

This 2008 edition published by Barnes & Noble, Inc.,
by arrangement with HarperCollins Publishers.

Barnes & Noble, Inc.
122 Fifth Avenue
New York, NY 10011

First published in 2004 by HarperCollins Publishers.

HarperCollins books may be purchased for educational, business, or
sales promotional use. For information, please write: Special Markets
Department, HarperCollins Publishers Inc., 10 East 53rd Street,
New York, NY 10022.

ISBN 13: 978-1-4351-0649-9
ISBN 10: 1-4351-0649-0

08 09 10 11 12 RRD 10 9 8 7 6 5 4 3 2 1

CONTENTS

INTRODUCTION

"There are mysteries connected with the birth of this Republic," wrote the American army officer Charles A. L. Totten, in 1897. Totten had come face-to-face with such mysteries while researching the history of the Great Seal of the United States. One mystery, which intrigued Totten above all others, was the origin of the magical symbolism of the Seal. He traced this mystery to 1776, when the design of the Great Seal was put in the capable hands of Thomas Jefferson, John Adam, and Benjamin Franklin. It was a mystery that had not been fully revealed, over a century later, when Totten published his book on the subject. It is a mystery that is still with us, even today.

Since the design of the familiar modern dollar bill is based on the symbols of this Great Seal, it is reasonable to amend Totten's words: *There are mysteries connected with the design of the dollar bill.*

Charles A. L. Totten was by no means the first American to recognize that the Great Seal had been designed on spiritual principles. Nor was he the first to recognize the depth of its secret symbolism, or to link this symbolism with biblical texts. He was, however, the first to write a comprehensive history of the Seal, incorporating a study of these hidden symbols. This it how it happened that the first serious study of the Great Seal of America was written, not by a professional historian, but by an officer of the American army. Totten equated the birth of the United States with the beginnings of what he called the *New Atlantis*—a title given to a work by Francis Bacon, one of the mysterious financial backers of the Virginia colony, in the early seventeenth century. Totten's vision was both mystical and vast, for it stretched from the mythological beginnings of America into the distant future, when, he believed, the spiritual achievements of the United States will be recognized by the world.

Because he was an amateur historian himself, it was only natural for him to appreciate the virtue of amateurism. While writing his history of the Seal, Totten pointed out that, so far as the design of the Great Seal was concerned, the Founding Fathers had been amateurs. Heraldry had not been one of their strong points. No doubt this was all to the good, for heraldry deals with the past—with bloodlines and aristocratic privilege—the very things against which the early republicans had fought. Even so, the Founding Fathers and the bevy of official helpers who gave us the Seal were the most ardent students of the inner spirit behind heraldry. This interest in a higher symbolism is reflected in the national Seal, and—by extension—in the dollar bill.

The dollar bill owes a great deal of its symbolism to the Great Seal of America—the design of which has evolved for over two centuries. The design of this Seal—and those symbols on the dollar bill that were derived from it—has gained a reputation for its magical content. As we shall see, not all this reputation is deserved. Even so, there may be no doubt that the Great Seal and the dollar bill represent the most extraordinary example in history of the public evolution of a magical design.

It is not always easy to trace the evolution of this design. Many of the early documents relating to the design of the Great Seal have survived and may be examined in public archives. The historic Seals themselves, after long use in public government, have found their way into the public archives of America institutions. Much of the documentation survives, yet behind this documentation there is a tantalizing opacity. The Seal and the dollar bill certainly contain magic symbols, yet it is not a matter of public record as to whence these symbols were derived or who introduced them to the roundels. Indeed, it is not always clear to what extent those who introduced them recognized their *magical* or *esoteric* content. In this fact lies the unanswered question pertaining to the secret of the dollar bill. Who did ensure that a piece of paper, designed for the most casual and ephemeral transactions, should have been a repository of an arcane and magical knowledge?

There are some who claim the Great Seal to be entirely a product of a secret school, intent on ensuring that every detail within its complex design had a magical quality about it. Such claims may be excessive and, even were they true, the identity of this secret school would still remain shrouded in mystery. The sources of these symbols may have been lost, and it may be an idle attempt to trace them to the arcane sources of the Freemasons, Rosicrucians, or other secret schools. Even so, the magical ideas that stemmed from these sources still live on. As we shall learn in the following pages, the two roundels of the pyramid and eagle, which now figure on the dollar bill, *are* replete with a magical significance that almost beggars belief.

The magic of the dollar bill resides in its ancient symbols, numerologies, and hidden alignments. These magical elements may be traced back to the curious fact that the Seal was designed by a number of different individuals during a period of over a century. In the course of the past two centuries, a large number of designers—many of them well aware of the nature of magical symbols—have contributed to the evolution of the Seal. A few of these designers have been impelled, by their own inner convictions, to add subtle touches to the national symbols in order to bring these in line with what they themselves believe to be the truth about the destiny of America.

If the design of the dollar bill is complex, the tradition of magic symbolism is even more complex. For this reason, I have tried to approach each of the magical symbols on the bill in a very simple way. Anyone who is interested in exploring more fully the points I raise may find the sequence of explanatory notes of some value. This is by no means intended to be an academic book, yet I feel that when one is making claims about so sacred and important a symbol as the dollar bill, one should be prepared to substantiate such claims—if only with sources and suggestions for further reading.

One should bear in mind that the dollar bill was designed for more reasons than to be the receptacle of magical power.

It was designed to be a currency—the lifeblood of the nation. The banking methods that lie behind the issue and maintenance of currency require that each note be marked with its source, date of issue, and an identification code. In turn, this means that some of the figures, numbers, codes, and letters on the dollar bill are ephemeral. These play no part in my numerical analyses. This must be understood, for otherwise, some of the claims I make about the symbolism of the bill may sound questionable. For example, in one part of my analysis I dwell on the number of times the individual figure 1 appears on the face of the note. The note I have before me, as I write, is one I obtained in Washington, D.C., in 1995. This has the series number 1995, the stamp of the Federal Reserve Bank of Richmond, Virginia, and a variety of other bank code numbers and letters that must be ignored, inasmuch as they are not designed to augment the magical design of the note itself. What I claim about the magical background to the dollar bill would be regarded as being nonsensical if one took into account such ephemeral things as the serial number, which includes the year.

Magic does not concern itself with ephemeral matters, but rather with those things that will endure the vicissitudes of time. Although the dollar bill enshrines that sacred date of 1776 in Roman numerals, its essential symbolism is designed to regard that date merely as a starting point. If we are to read the symbolism of the dollar bill aright, this was the year in which began the great experiment in nation building. It was the beginning of a time from which America began to look forward to a New Age during which, with the aid of God, one great nation would grow from the many. When that enterprise is completed, then the symbol of the truncated pyramid will become history. The pyramid will have been completed and will endure upon that sound base first laid down in 1776 by men who were giants, whose lengthened shadows now form our own history.

For legal and technical reasons, it has not proved possible to reproduce the dollar bill in any other form than drawings. In some ways, this is all to the good: the dollar bill is an exquisite example of quality engraving, and no reproduction can do justice to the precision of its design. Indeed, it was designed in a way intended to make reproduction difficult. Even the good-quality artwork that has been used in this book cannot measure up to the precision of the original dollar bill. For this reason, when one is called upon to make special measurements, or to lay straight edges along the design, to examine the amazing secret relationships of certain forms, it is essential that this be done directly on a genuine dollar bill rather than on the artwork provided here. If such measurements *are* made directly on the artwork, there may be minute deviations such as will not be found on the dollar bill itself.

The only thing needed to explore the following pages is a sample of the dollar bill. Everything I claim about its magical structure and design should be checked carefully against this *real* object rather than merely against the diagrams within this book.

Finally, I must explain that I have left the enduring mystery of the dollar bill until the last section. The magic symbolism of the bill is so profound that, if one is to fully appreciate its subtleties, a certain insight into such a symbolism is required. Without such an insight, it is unlikely that the full significance of the bill will be observed. Unless one can grasp the meaning of the radiant light above the truncated pyramid . . . . Unless one has some knowledge of the pagan Egyptian triangle . . . Unless one has some awareness of the mystery of the Christian number 33 . . . Then there is little hope that one may begin to appreciate the profound mystery of the two magical roundels on the dollar bill. It is for this reason that I have left the most outstanding secret of the dollar bill to the last section, by which time we should have begun to appreciate the magic of the radiant light, the triangle, and the number 33.

The DOLLAR

1. The symbol $ for the dollar does not appear on the dollar bill.

It is a curious fact that the official symbol for the dollar, $, does not appear on the bill. The word DOLLAR appears only twice—once on either side of the note.

2. The word *dollar* came to America from Germany.

The word *dollar* is derived from the German *taler*. The name *taler* was first given to silver coins made in 1519. This metal was mined in Joachimsthal (Joachim's valley, or *thaler*), in what was then Bohemia.

The obverse of one thaler showed the crucified Christ. On the reverse was the image of a serpent, hanging from a cross.

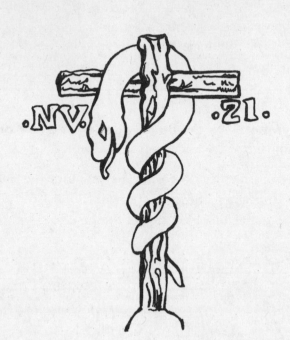

Near the serpent's head are the two letters NU, and on the other side of the cross, the number 21. This is a reference to Numbers, chapter 21, of the Bible.

In this chapter, we learn of the people of Israel who began to speak against God because of their tribulations and because they feared that they would die in the wilderness. As punishment, God sent against them fiery serpents. These bit many of the Israelites, as a result of which a number died. The people of Israel recognized their sin and begged for forgiveness. God instructed Moses to make a fiery serpent and set it upon a pole. Thereafter, anyone who looked upon that image would be cured. Moses did as he was ordered and raised a brazen serpent on a pole; all those who gazed upon it lived. It is this healing metal serpent that is shown on the reverse of the thaler.

In this image, the pole has become a cross, as the artist wished to draw a parallel between the magical healing power of this brass serpent and the healing power of Christ, who hung upon the cross.

It is this origin that has led some historians to claim that the thaler image of the serpent-cross is the origin for the dollar sign,

The idea that the dollar symbol was derived from the cross of Christ was remembered in American literature in 1920, fifteen years before the new dollar bill was designed.

In his novel *Main Street*, Sinclair Lewis reports a conversation between "the half-Yank and half-Swede," Bjornstam and the heroine of the novel, Carol. Bjornstam, lamenting the power of bankers, points out that the dollar sign has "chased the crucifix clean off the map." This half-joke would have meaning only for those who knew that the dollar sign, $, had been derived from a crucifix: a few lines later on, Bjornstam admitted that he was a bookworm.

3. The word *dollar* was in use in English at the beginning of the seventeenth century.

The word *dollar* was used in an English translation of a survey of the kingdoms of the world published in 1603. This part of the text (below) deals with the kingdom of what was then called *Hungerland*, or Hungary. The word *dollars* appears in the last full line, below.

> This aſſembly is ſtil in vſe,but the freedome therof is altered, no-thing being at this day propounded vnto the aſſembled by the archduke Mathias,the emperors viceroy,but a contribution of mo-ny, to which demand at a day giuen, the nobility giue their reſolu-tion which in the year 96.and 97.when the turkiſh emperor thret-ned to deſcend himſelfe in perſon,was, that the nobility wold put themſelues in Campania with their forces, and promiſed for their ſubieꝯs (for ſo they tearme their peaſants) that euery houſhoulder ſhould ſend a man and giue 2.dollars of money for entertainment of ſouldiers;

4. The symbol $ was being widely used in America at the end of the eighteenth century.

The Continental Congress, following the advise of Thomas Jefferson, adopted the dollar as the money unit of the United States in 1785. In his own report, Jefferson had used a variant of the symbol ' for the dollar.

At that time, there were a number of ways of writing the symbol, and not everyone used these symbols. For example, in correspondence relating to the Continental currency printed in 1797, the English pound symbol £ was used, yet the dollar was symbolized by the letter D. In an official tariff of import duties published in 1824, the symbol $ was used.

5. The symbol $ may have been derived from the alchemical tradition.

The biblical story of the brazen serpent (see 2) had impressed the alchemists long before the thaler was minted.

In consequence, the alchemists often represented the brazen serpent in their works, in both pictorial and symbolic forms. One of the symbolic forms, which was linked with the idea of healing, was represented as follows:

This was a version of brazen serpent represented as a curvilinear line on a tau cross. Since the brazen serpent image appeared on the thaler (the original dollar), then it follows that the symbol ₮ may have been the origin of the modern symbol for the dollar, the now familiar $.

6. The original name *dollar* was linked with a holy number.

In the medieval period, each letter of the alphabet was associated with a particular number. Every word had a particular numerical value made from the addition of the letter-numbers in that word.

For example, the Hebrew word for the serpent of Moses was written נחש and had the sound *Nachash*. The numerical equivalent of this word was:

$$
\begin{aligned}
N &= 50 \\
Ch &= 8 \\
Sh &= 300 \\
TOTAL &= 358
\end{aligned}
$$

This means that the numerical equivalent of the serpent of Moses was 358.

Now, the number of the Hebrew word for the Messiah (which was written משיח and which has the sound *MshIch*) was also 358.

$$M = 40$$
$$Sh = 300$$
$$I = 10$$
$$Ch = 8$$
$$TOTAL = 358$$

This correspondence between the numerical equivalents of the two words allowed magicians to draw a connection between the brazen serpent and the Messiah. Just as the serpent of the Old Testament was raised on a pole to heal the Israelites, so was the Messiah raised on a cross to heal the world.

This view of numerical symbolism explains why the brazen serpent image used by the alchemists, ₴, was regarded with particular veneration. Besides being an image of the healing serpent, it was also a portrayal of Christ on the cross.

In numerology, one is allowed to "reduce" numbers. That is to say, one adds the numbers together as individual units to obtain a second figure. If you add together 358, you obtain 16. There are sixteen words in the two roundel designs of the dollar bill, counting the Latin date on the bottom of the pyramid:

ANNUIT CŒPTIS—2 words
MCCCLXXVI—1 word

NOVUS ORDO SECLORUM—3 words
THE GREAT SEAL—3 words
E PLURIBUS UNUM—3 words
OF THE UNITED STATES—4 words

If you further reduce the number 16, you obtain 7. There are seven words beneath the two roundels (THE GREAT SEAL OF THE UNITED STATES). The word ONE appears seven times on the back of the dollar bill (the Latin *unum* in the eagle roundel motto means "one").

In magical numerology, the number 7 is regarded with especial veneration. It is a deeply religious number, representing the triumph of spirit (3) over matter (4). Certain texts that deal with the meanings of numbers insist that 7 "stands for the complete temple." There is a connection between the "complete temple" and the "uncompleted pyramid" of the dollar-bill roundel.

7. It is possible that the dollar symbol, $, was derived from astrology.

The medieval astrologers sometimes used the symbol $ to denote the planet Mercury—the planet that had rule over such things as commerce. The form of this symbol is said to have been derived from the image of a snake curling along a rod or staff. Two versions of this early symbolism are as follows:

The wand, or caduceus, carried by the god Mercury consisted of a rod with *two* serpents curled around it:

According to the astrological tradition, Mercury ruled
finance, banking, and so on, so it is not at all unreasonable
that the symbol should be used to denote currency.

The sixteenth-century woodcut above shows Mercury
holding a pair of serpents in his right hand and a bag of
money in his left. The serpents are intended as reference to
the caduceus, the bag of money to Mercury's rule over
banking, commerce, and financial transactions.

It is traditional for banks to have sculpted models of
either Mercury or the caduceus on their façades or doors.
The Bank of England, in London, has a caduceus on either
of the main doors. Above the main portal of the Federal
Reserve Building, in Washington, D.C., is a sculpture of a
female personification of America, holding a caduceus. This
was sculpted in 1937, two years after the modern dollar bill
was designed and printed.

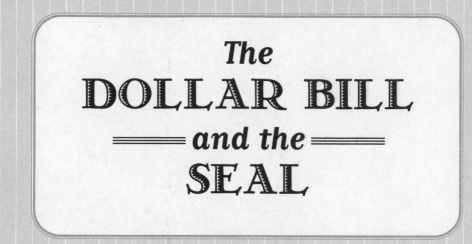

The
DOLLAR BILL
and the
SEAL

8. The two roundels on the dollar bill are based on the designs for the Great Seal of the United States.

In 1935, Franklin D. Roosevelt ordered that a new dollar bill should be designed. He requested that this design should be based on the symbolism of the Great Seal of America.

This design was executed by Edward M. Weeks, of the Bureau of Engraving and Printing.

The obverse of this was the famous American eagle, with the shield at its breast. The reverse was the equally famous pyramid design. Both of these designs contained magical and Masonic symbols, and Roosevelt was aware of this.

As we have seen, the dollar bill itself informs us that the pyramid and eagle roundels are derived from the Great Seal of America. Beneath the two roundels on the dollar bill is a broken inscription. Beneath the pyramid roundel are the words THE GREAT SEAL. Beneath the eagle roundel are the words OF THE UNITED STATES.

9. The designer of the dollar bill had no official model for the pyramid roundel.

By 1935, there were in existence several versions of the Great Seal, each containing minor variations of symbolism. The designer of the bill, Edward M. Weeks, selected that version of the eagle roundel that was currently in use. This particular version had been in official use since 1904.

However, the reverse of the Seal (that is, the pyramid roundel) had never been used in official business, and no die for this design existed (see, however, page 106). Accordingly, the designer selected, as a basis for his new dollar bill, a *painting* of the reverse. This had been reproduced in an official book dealing with the history of the Seal, and published in 1909. Drawings based on the two designs for the Seal, from this 1909 source, are given below:

These may be compared with the two dollar-bill roundels above, in 8. If you examine the four roundels carefully, you will see some important differences between the Seal design and the roundel of the dollar bill. Some of the more important differences are listed on pages 157–58.

10. The dollar bill of 1935 was designed by Freemasons.

The most influential men involved in the design of the dollar bill of 1935 were Freemasons. Among these was the President of the United States, Franklin D. Roosevelt; the Secretary of Agriculture, Henry A. Wallace; and the Secretary of the Treasury, Henry Morgenthau. All three were Masons.

The Masonic interest in symbols may explain why the dollar bill was carefully designed to convey a wide range of secret symbolism. As we shall discover, among these Masonic symbols are the radiant eye (above the truncated pyramid) and the five-pointed star.

11. The two roundels were made part of the design of the dollar bill in 1935.

The suggestion that the roundels should be used on the dollar bill appears to have come from the future vice president of the United States, Henry A. Wallace.

Wallace's suggestion was accepted. The President of the United States officially approved the design for the dollar bill on or near July 1, 1935. Below is a copy of Franklin D. Roosevelt's personal suggestions for changing the order of the two roundels, so that the eagle roundel would appear on the right.

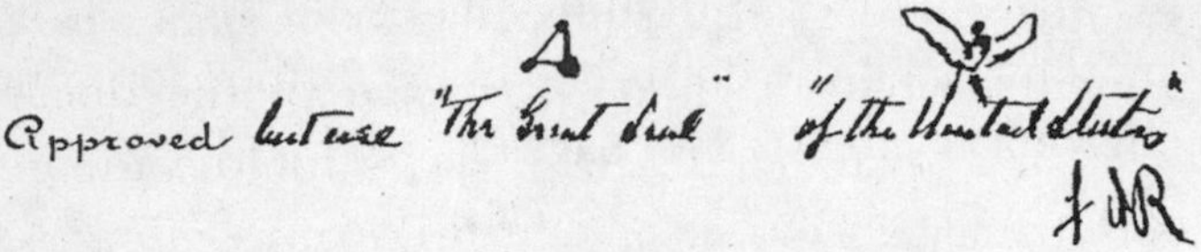

12. The identity of the designer of the Great Seal is not known.

It has never been possible to ascribe the design of the Great Seal to any particular individual. The design for the shield evolved over a number of years, during which time different symbols and designs were proposed by a number of individuals. The original design was discussed and considered by at least a dozen officials (including men of such standing as Benjamin Franklin and Thomas Jefferson).

Even after the first die for the Seal was cut in 1782, the design was not completed according to the instructions given by Congress.

As we shall see, the three men who contributed most to the design of the Seal were William Barton of Pennsylvania, the Secretary of Congress Charles Thomson, and the artist Pierre Eugène Du Simitière.

13. The design of the Seal evolved, with the passing of the years.

From time to time, the design for the Great Seal was amended.

Each time a die wore out, changes were made to the original design—some of them for the worse, some for the better. Below, we shall examine the main stages in these adjustments, which lead to the design of the dollar bill roundels. For the moment, it may be useful to compare the earliest official Seal obverse with the corresponding design on the modern dollar bill.

14.The first metal die for the Great Seal was cut in 1782.

It was quite reasonable that the design for the Seal should have been the work of a committee and the result of the meeting of many minds. However, the cutting of the die for the Seal, to make from it a metal impress, could have been the work of only one man. The identity of this individual is not known for sure. However, it seems likely that it was cut by Robert Scot, in Philadelphia, in 1782.

Scot was a Mason. This may explain certain curious things about the design of the first Seal. It contains several symbols derived from the magical tradition. As we shall see, most of these symbols were transmitted to the design of the dollar bill.

If we are to understand the source of the secret symbolism of the dollar bill, we must examine the major changes in the Seal design. Altogether, there were four different Seal designs adopted for official use in the United States. The earliest design was that of 1782. The fourth design, officially adopted in 1904, was the basis for the eagle roundel on the dollar bill. In the next sections, we shall examine the designs for the four historic Seals.

15. The first design for the Great Seal—1782.

In the Seal of 1782, some effort was made to make use of the number 13—the number of original colonies to oppose Britain. Whoever cut the die for the Great Seal appears to have been the first to arrange the thirteen stars in the starlike pattern above the head of the eagle.

The eagle grasps thirteen arrows in its left talon. However, the olive branch, in its right talon, consists of sixteen leaves. The wings of the eagle, which might easily have consisted of thirteen feathers, were built up from eleven to the right of the eagle and twelve to the left.

The stars on this first Great Seal of 1782 were six-pointed. By a strange coincidence, a drawing made of the Seal for the *Columbian Magazine* in 1786 portrayed thirteen five-pointed stars around the head of the eagle (below).

The Seal of the United States was first used on an official document dated September 16, 1782. This document authorized George Washington to negotiate with the British and to sign an agreement for the exchange and treatment of prisoners of war.

The symbolism of the 13 arrows is often misunderstood. They are not intended as symbols of aggression—as the darker side of the olive-bearing coin. In Charles Thomson's report on the design of the Seal, it is made clear that the arrows and olive branch represent the power of peace and war exclusively vested in Congress. Their heraldic meaning is that the United States will only go to war after provocation. They are *Jonathan arrows*—intended as a shot across the bows of any threatening enemy.

16. The seal design of 1841.

The Seal of 1782 was used until 1841, by which time it was so badly worn that it needed replacing. The worn original is now in the National Archives, in Washington, D.C.

A new die was cut in 1841 by John Peter Van Ness Throop, then living in Washington, D.C.

The stars on this seal were changed, so as to become five-pointed. The eagled grasped only six arrows in its talons. There were seventeen leaves on the olive branch. The long feathers of the eagle's wings were still unevenly distributed. The right wing had fourteen end feathers: the left wing had fifteen.

17. The Seal design of 1877.

The Seal of 1841 was used until 1877, when it began to show signs of wear. The Seal of 1877 was cut by the German engraver Herman Baumgarten, who lived in Washington, D.C. This Seal closely resembled that of 1841.

18. The Seal design of 1885.

In 1885, the firm of Tiffany & Company, in collaboration with many advisers and historians, designed a new Seal. This design corrected several errors that had crept into the Seal as early as 1783.

The most important of these changes were as follows The stars were retained as five-pointed. There were now thirteen leaves on the olive branch and thirteen berries on the same branch. There were thirteen arrows in the talons of the eagle. The eagle was clearly represented as the American bald-headed eagle. The clouds around the constellation formed a complete ring around the glory.

19. The Seal of 1904

In 1904, a new die was cut by Max Zeitler. In order to reveal the heraldic colors that had been specified for the design of 1782, but not incorporated into the Seal, Zeitler changed the design of the radiants around the stars.

In the place of the sixty-five radiants that appeared in the Tiffany design, Zeitler introduced twenty-five line radiants and as many broken (dotted lines). Some of these consisted of two dots, others of three. Altogether there were fifty-five dots and twenty-five lines on this glory. A drawing is reproduced below.

This design was the basis for the eagle roundel in the dollar bill.

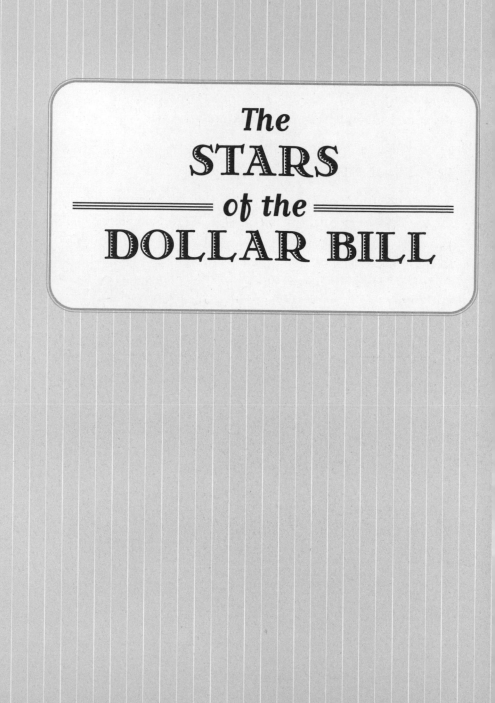

The STARS of the DOLLAR BILL

20. There are thirteen stars on the face of the dollar bill.

There are thirteen stars on the face of the dollar bill. However, these are not so evident as those on the constellation above the eagle on the back of the bill. They are located on the chevron of the seal of the Department of the Treasury Seal, printed over the top of the ONE, to the left of Washington's portrait.

This seal (above) contains a balance and a key—both appropriate symbols for a Treasury Department: the starry chevron is an obvious reference to the country that the balance and key serve.

21. There are fourteen stars on the back of the dollar bill.

It is widely believed that there are thirteen stars on the back of the dollar bill, above the head of the eagle. In fact, there are really fourteen stars. The thirteen five-pointed stars are arranged in such a way as to form a six-pointed star.

This geometric arrangement of thirteen stars is not the only one possible. For example, the Confederatio copper coin, minted in 1785, represents the group of thirteen in the form of two superimposed crosses.

In effect, this "constellation" has the appearance of being an eight-pointed star.

The important thing is that the eight-pointed arrangement has no particularly important magical associations,
whereas the six-pointed arrangement found on the dollar
bill does have such associations.

The thirteen five-pointed stars within the constellation
arrangement above the head of the dollar eagle are all
arranged so that their points are *upright*. In books of popular
magic, it is sometimes claimed that the *inverted* star, or pentacle, ✩, is a sign of evil—that it is a bringer of bad fortune.
This idea is nonsensical. Examples of inverted five-pointed
stars are found in many works of art in several American
cities, including the nation's capital, Washington, D.C.

There are several examples on the bronze frieze, sculpted

THALES

by Laurie Lee, in 1923, on the façade of the National Academy of Sciences Building, in Washington, D.C. Two inverted stars may be seen above the Egyptian pyramid, above the head of the Greek philosopher, Thales, and two more at the feet of Euclid and Democritus, behind Thales.

These stars alternate with solar symbols along the frieze. Each sun has thirteen main radiants, with thirteen subsidary radiants peeping out between the larger ones. Below is a detail of the frieze, from beneath the left foot of Thales.

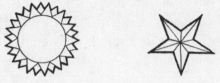

22. The group of thirteen stars above the head of the eagle are based on a magical symbol.

As we have seen, the thirteen stars above the dollar eagle have been so arranged as to represent two interlocked triangles:

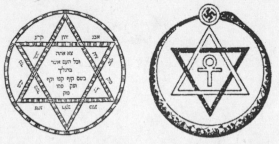

This is the Seal of Solomon or Star of David—a symbol that is widely used in magical texts under a variety of magical names.

The symbolism of this star is just a little deeper than one

might at first imagine. The outer points number six. The word *dollar* has six letters. The word one appears on this side of the dollar bill six times.

The inner spaces of the Seal of Solomon number seven. This is the same number as the words appearing in THE GREAT SEAL OF THE UNITED STATES beneath the two roundels. It is also the same as the number of letters in the word AMERICA. It is also the same as the number of words in the two roundels, if we count the Latin date. It is also the same as the number of words at the top and bottom of the roundel face: THE UNITED STATES OF AMERICA and ONE DOLLAR.

23. The stars on the first design of the Great Seal had six points.

The chief difference between the eagle roundel on the dollar bill and the eagle on the first Great Seal (1782) was in the number of radiants or points on the stars above the head of the eagle. On the dollar-bill roundel, the thirteen stars have five radiants. The thirteen stars on the Great Seal of 1782 had six radiants.

The majority of states that made use of the stars in their official seals insisted on five-pointed stars. An outstanding example is the seal of Oklahoma, the central device of which consists of a large encircled five-pointed star on a ground set with five groups of nine stars—forty-five in all. The total number of stars is intended to commemorate the fact that it was the forty-sixth state.

24. The stars and stripes on the dollar bill are *not* derived from the coat of arms of George Washington.

The ancient arms of the Washington family are still preserved in several places in England. These arms display the stars and stripes, which many people believe was the source of the stars and stripes of the American flag.

The example below is copied from the one carved in stone, above the front entrance of Sulgrave Manor (Northamptonshire), which was formerly owned by Lawrence Washington, one of George Washington's forebears. Lawrence had purchased the land from King Henry VIII

and built upon it the existing manor.

This arms display five-pointed stars (in heraldry called mullets) and two horizontal stripes or bars. The arms, adopted for George Washington's personal bookplate, are shown alongside. These might have influenced the designs of late-eighteenth-century American coinage. However, the fact that the stars on the original design of the Seal were six-pointed rules out the Washington arms as a source for the stars that appeared on the Great Seal.

As a matter of fact, the early interest in six-pointed stars never entirely died out in American symbolism. For example, the seal of the state of Maryland (used until 1854) centered on a shield-bearing eagle over the head of which is an arc of thirteen stars. These stars are six-pointed (see below).

The great star, in which this roundel is set, has thirteen radiants.

25. The symbolism of the stars on the dollar bill.

When the stars were first used on the proposed design for the Great Seal, the Secretary of the Continental Congress, Charles Thomson, referred to them as "a constellation."

These first appeared in a sketch on page 32 for the Seal, drawn personally by Thomson:

We see that the thirteen stars are six-pointed and are represented in a disorderly fashion above the head of the eagle.

By this time, a "constellation of stars" was already being used as symbols of the United States. A number of coins had already been minted with a constellation of thirteen stars around a radiant star of thirteen points. In the center of one, minted about 1783 (below), is an eye. The Latin on this coin, *Constellatio Nova*, means "New Constellation."

No doubt this was intended to suggest that the United States was a new constellation of stars suddenly appearing in the skies. These origins suggest that the thirteen small stars on the dollar bill are intended to represent the United

States as a new constellation in the sky. It is this interpretation that leads us to another interesting connection that the dollar bill has with magic symbolism.

26. The earliest five-pointed star.

The earliest known use of the five-pointed star was in ancient Egypt. It was an hieroglyphic with the name *sba* and symbolized the spiritual world and the realm of stars.

The *sba* may be seen at the top of the central collection of hieroglyphics, above. This is the name of the goddess Isis, who is represented below the hieroglyphics. Further examples of *sba* stars are given on page 53.

The walls and ceilings of certain interior chambers in

some Egyptian pyramid chambers are entirely covered in bas-relief carvings of five-pointed *sba* stars.

27. The earliest known official use of the five-pointed star in North America.

The earliest official use of the five-pointed star in North America was on coinage introduced to the Bermudas in 1616.

All denominations of this coin had the image of a sailing ship on the reverse. On the obverse above was a hog. Around the hog was the inscription SOMMER ISLANDS, the seventeenth-century name of the Bermudas, and two five-pointed stars.

28. The five-pointed star and Francis Bacon.

The five-pointed star may have come to North America by way of the arms of Sir Francis Bacon, who knew William Shakespeare.

It is possible that both the hog and the five-pointed star

on the coin we have just examined were introduced from Sir Francis Bacon's coat of arms. At the time the hog money was made, Bacon was the attorney general of England: toward the end of 1616, he was appointed Lord Keeper of the Great Seal. The crest of this arms was a hog (a play on Bacon's name), and on the shield were two pairs of five-pointed stars:

William Shakespeare mentioned the Bermudas (which he called the Bermoothes) in his play *The Tempest*.

29. The five-pointed star in Florida.

The oldest known five-pointed star in the Americas appeared in a drawing of an event witnessed in Florida, made by a French artist.

This drawing, which has survived as a sixteenth-century

engraving, portrays a North American shaman, contorted in a trance, within a magic circle. At the forefront of the circle is a five-pointed star.

The drawing was turned into a painting by the French artist Jacques le Moyne de Morgue in about 1564, after he had returned from Florida and settled in England. The origi-

nal painting has been lost, but it was engraved and published in 1591. The detail on page 36 is from one of these engravings.

No doubt it is an accident that the outer edge of the modern official Seal of Florida should display a five-pointed star.

30. The idea of the "new constellation" of thirteen stars was probably derived from the design for the national flag, approved in 1777.

On June 14, 1777, Congress officially approved the design for a national flag, consisting of thirteen stripes, alternating red with white, and a union of thirteen white stars upon a blue background. The arrangement of thirteen stars on the Great Seal was probably suggested by this officially approved design.

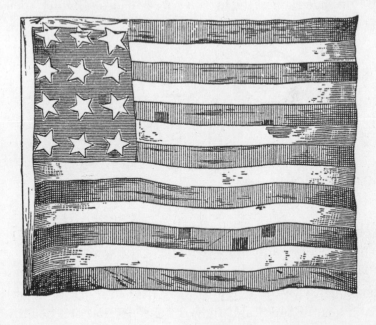

31. The five-pointed star is a magical symbol.

The five-pointed star is a powerful magical symbol with several meanings. It is associated with a healthy physical body and spirit. Here we shall examine only two of these meanings—we shall see how it is used as a symbol of health and how it is used to symbolize the passage of time.

The five-pointed pentacle was widely used as a symbol of health—or, more exactly, of those forces in the body that promoted health. This form of pentacle was popular during the Renaissance—especially as an amulet. Below is a woodcut showing an example of a ring, on the bezel of which has been engraved a five-pointed star. This star has been reproduced alongside, to show clearly the letters written around it. Alongside each of the five rays are five letters, which spell out the word *salus*, the Latin for "health."

Both star and word were designed to evoke their powers, to protect the health and well-being of the wearer.

The symbolism behind the five-lettered word *salus* was connected with the notion (widely held in magical circles) that a healthy physical body was the reflection of a healthy spirit. If the invisible spirit were morally "healthy," then the human body would be physically healthy. On this level, the five-pointed star represents the higher spirit. Perhaps this *salus* diagram (which is very ancient) is one reason why the Greek philosopher Pythagoras associated the number 5 with healing.

Since the name of Jesus has five letters, the early Christian numerologists recognized the power of the pentacle and used it as an amulet. The amulet below shows Jesus Christ standing in front of a pentacle.

This imagery (which portrayed Jesus as the great healer of mankind) was partly linked with the idea that the number 5 was also the number of rebirth or resurrection.

32. The five-pointed star is a magical symbol linked with duration and time.

The connection that the five-pointed star has with health and with the physical body is expressed in a multitude of magical diagrams. One image that was widely used by magicians was of the figure of a man inscribed within the pentagram. In such diagrams, each of the five points is related to one of the five "extremities" of the body—the head, hands, and feet.

In the diagram above, which is from a book on magic, published in 1534, each of the five points are also associated with one of the planets. Starting at the head, and working clockwise, these are:

Mars [♂]
Jupiter [♃]
Saturn [♄]
Mercury [☿], and
Venus [♀]

The sequence of planets, which emerges as one follows the lines of the pentagram, is designed to reflect the days of the week. Monday, or Moon Day, is marked by the crescent Moon [☽] at the center of the circle. The next day is found by following the vertical to the head, to reach Mars [♂], which represents Tuesday. By following the sequence of five lines, one passes through the order of planets that rule the days of the week. In some cases, the name of the day is associated with the name of a pagan god or goddess, as follows:

> Tiw's Day—Mars Day—Tuesday
> Woden's Day—Mercury Day—Wednesday
> Thor's Day—Jupiter Day—Thursday
> Freya's Day—Venus's Day—Friday
> Saturn's Day—Saturday.

To reach Sunday (literally, Sun's Day), you move from Saturn, up the center of the leg, to the symbol that represents the Sun, on the man's stomach [☉].

This is an example of how the magical pentagram, or five-pointed star, is linked in magic with *time*—that is, with the sequence of days.

33. The five-pointed stars, at the spiritual center of the United States, were intended to represent endless time and spirit.

It was at the suggestion of Jefferson Davis that the sculptor Thomas Crawford placed a circlet of stars around the head of the statue of *Freedom*, which was to stand on top of the Capitol Building in Washington, D.C. at the symbolic hub of the United States. Davis held the conviction that a circle of stars would symbolize "endless existence and heavenly birth." There is little evidence to suggest that Davis knew much about magic, but the fact is that, with this phrase, he has reached into the deep meaning of the five-pointed star in the arcane tradition.

There are nine stars around the helmet, each of them five-pointed. They measure just over 8½ inches at their widest points, and stand proud of the helmet's surface. The wood engraving (opposite) is from an early photograph that Thomas Crawford had taken in Rome, where he had sculpted the statue. This offers a much clearer view of the helmet than is possible from the grounds of the Capitol itself.

34. It has been suggested that the thirteen stars on the Seal and dollar bill represent a particular constellation.

In 1853, the American historian Schuyler Hamilton argued that the phrase "a constellation of stars" in the description of the Great Seal of the United States was intended to point to a particular constellation. He was convinced that this constellation was Lyra, the stellar Harp in the grasp of the Eagle. The following image of the Eagle and Lyra, reproduced on the following page, appeared on the title page of the book that Hamilton wrote about the subject.

Hamilton came to the conclusion that America should be identified with the prime star in Lyra, which was Wega. This star is among the brightest in the skies.

On the harp of Lyra (page 44) is a constellation of stars, the brightest of which (between the head and left wing of the Eagle) has eight rays, to identify it as Wega. Hamilton saw this prime star—the "leading star" of Lyra—as being the equivalent of America leading the whole world.

Schuyler Hamilton had been encouraged to identify the star of America by the former Secretary of State, John Quincy Adams, who was interested in astronomy and astrology. In 1820, Adams had designed a device for a new American passport. This incorporated a circle of stars

around the stellar Eagle, which held in its beak the constellation Lyra. The device was similar to that which Hamilton used on the title page of his own book (reproduced above). The motto *Nunc Sidera Ducit* ("Now it leads the stars") was a reference to America leading all the other stars, as they circle the heavens.

The EYE Of PROVIDENCE

35. The Eye of Providence was first introduced to the Great Seal by a Swiss artist.

The Swiss artist Du Simitière was an acquaintance of Benjamin Franklin, Thomas Jefferson, and John Adams. Perhaps because of these connections, he was invited to work as the official artist for the committee set up by Congress to propose designs for the Great Seal. He was the first to sketch a design that included the image of an eye within a triangle. Benjamin Franklin, who was on the First Committee, may have suggested this idea to him. Du Simitière's sketch has survived, and is reproduced here:

Franklin was a leading Mason and may have suggested the Eye of Providence because it was widely used as a Masonic symbol. Among the many symbols used by Masons was the "blazing star," which was a five-pointed radiant star.

In some radiant stars was the G for Geometry (below, left). In others was an eye, within a radiant triangle (below, right).

In the written description that accompanied the sketch, the artist referred to the eye as 'the Eye of Providence in a radiant Triangle." This was widely used as a Masonic symbol. Below is an early-nineteenth-century Masonic symbol that combines the blazing star with the letter G (for Geometry) *and* an Eye of Providence.

36. The first proposal for the Eye of Providence represented it as a left eye.

The engraving on the following page was made in 1856. It is an interpretation, made by the artist, Benson J. Lossing, of the Du Simitière proposal of 1776 for the design of the Great Seal.

This depicts an eye in a radiant triangle. In the original drawing, Barton had marked out the triangle with a line. In this engraving, the triangle is picked out in white, by the radiants.

The eye itself is from the left-hand side of the face.

37. The Eye of Providence, which appeared in later designs for the Seal, was a right eye.

In 1782, William Barton had sketched a proposed design for the reverse of the Great Seal. This consisted of an unfinished pyramid, with thirteen levels, surrounded by a motto and topped by a radiant eye.

The eye drawn by Barton is clearly a *right* eye.

The two Latin mottoes proposed by Barton are: *Deo Favente* ("With God's Favor") and *Perennis* ("Enduring through the years").

38. The eye on the dollar bill is from the left side of the face.

The eye within the radiant triangle in the dollar-bill roundel is a left eye.

It seems that the final design of the truncated pyramid was more influenced by the original idea proposed by the Swiss artist Du Simitière.

In the magical tradition, the left eye is linked with the Moon and the right eye with the Sun.

39. The eye above the unfinished pyramid on the dollar bill could be of Egyptian origin.

Among the many thousands of paintings that have survived in Egyptian papyrus rolls, and inside the walls of tombs, is a picture of a pyramid below a pair of eyes.

In ancient Egypt, the chief god was called Asari (the Greeks called him Osiris). The name was written in Egyptian hieroglyphics as:

The two hieroglyphics mean "throne" and "see." Osiris was the all-seeing god, and his eye appears in a multitude of Egyptian art forms, of which the above painting is typical. As we shall see, on the surface of a surviving capstone of an Egyptian pyramid (called a *ben-ben*) were two eyes.

The eye above the pyramid on the dollar-bill roundel is set within a triangle, which reminds one of the capstone of a pyramid. However, this triangle is surrounded by a brilliant aura that seems to represents either the Sun or the spiritual world.

The image of an eye within a triangle was used by Masons long before the Great Seal of 1782 was designed. It is highly likely that this eye was derived from Egyptian symbolism.

The Eye of Providence, or the Eye of God, which appeared in Christian art, was probably derived from early Egyptian imagery relating to the god Osiris.

40. The eye was an important magical symbol during the Renaissance.

In the fifteenth century, the Italian poet Francesco Colonna made an attempt to translate the Egyptian hieroglyphics. He interpreted the image of the eye below as representing God or Divine Justice. This interpretation was, of course,

very close to the idea of the Eye of Providence now on the dollar bill.

As it happened, the hieroglyphic of the eye meant no such thing, but Colonna's proposal was soon widely accepted by scholars. Colonna's idea spread throughout Europe and the Americas, in both secular and church art. This is why the image of the radiant eye was adopted in the centuries afterwards, as meaning God or Providence.

41. The eye of the Sun is found in Egyptian symbolism.

In ancient Egyptian symbolism, the right eye was a symbol of the sun god Osiris. Perhaps this explains why Barton enclosed his eye in a radiant sunburst.

In the Egyptian drawing below, there are two eyes—one from the left-hand side of the face, the other from the right.

The sacred baboon is handing back to the Moon god his own eye, which in the myth had been swallowed by a demon. Because this is the eye of the Moon, it is from the left side of the face. Painted on the prow of the boat at the foot of the baboon is the eye of the Sun—a right-hand eye.

The twenty-four stars that run along the base of this drawing are examples of the five-pointed *sba* star, so important in Egyptian symbolism.

42. The radiant triangle of the dollar bill is intended to complete the truncated pyramid.

The triangle, with its enclosed eye, completes the truncated pyramid of the dollar bill.

The symbolism is designed to suggest that the pyramid will be completed with the aid of the all-seeing God. This idea is expressed in the motto above the pyramid (see below). It is also hinted at in the national motto of the United States, "In God We Trust" (see page 89).

43. The eye of God, which is on the dollar bill, was from an ancient magical tradition.

The Freemasons were the most influential body to adopt the eye as a symbol of God or the Supreme Being. As we have seen, they sometimes enclosed the image of the eye in a triangle to suggest the idea of the Trinity, or Three in One.

The seventeenth-century German mystic Jacob Boehme introduced many symbols that were later adopted into the Masonic tradition. Among these symbols was the eye, as a representative of the Godhead. In the sample plate below, the eye is at the center of a burning triangle.

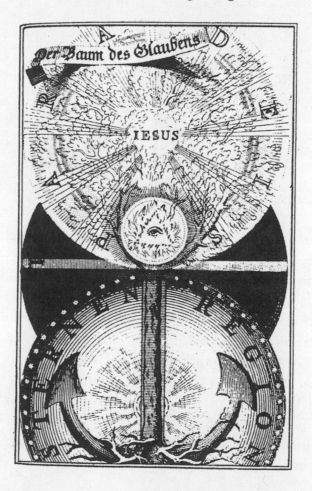

The circle, which contains the flaming triangle, forms the top of an anchor. This anchor links the light world of Jesus with the star world (the *sternen region*) below.

Just as the triangle of the dollar bill completes the pyramid below, so the flaming triangle in this illustration completes the anchor below. If you draw two lines that continue the slopes of the flaming triangles, you will find that they just enclose the grappling arcs of the anchor.

On one level of symbolism, the threefold spiritual triangle (the Trinity) is linked with the threefold structure of the anchor. On another level of symbolism, the spiritual fire of the triangle is linked with the visible fire of the stars.

There is another interesting link with this magical symbolism and the dollar bill. The periphery of the lower circle, which surrounds the anchor, is marked with thirty-two stars. Behind the anchor is the Sun, another star, making thirty-three stars in all. This is a magical number because it is the total number of years that Jesus Christ spent on the earth. Eventually, we shall discover that this magical hidden meaning is linked with the symbolism of the dollar bill.

44. The eye of God and the five-pointed star were early Masonic symbols.

One of the earliest uses of the radiant eye of God, alongside a five-pointed star, was by a seventeenth century Scottish Mason. Sir Robert Moray had the radiant eye and five-pointed star carved for use as a private seal. This seal has been preserved on a letter from Robert Moray to the Earl of Essex, now in the British Library, London. The red wax seal is broken, and part of it is missing, but both the radiant eye and the five-pointed star are still visible:

Moray made extensive use of the five-pointed star. For example, he used it at a final flourish on his personal signature.

Moray may have been the Mason who popularized both the radiant eye and the five-pointed star among the English Masons. Perhaps, indeed, one or both of these symbols were introduced indirectly into America during his lifetime. The earliest known Freemasons in America were John Forbes and John Skene, who emigrated to New Jersey in the 1680s. They had been members of the Aberdeen Lodge, in Scotland, and cannot fail to have been aware of the symbolism that fascinated Robert Moray.

45. The eye of God, within a ring of clouds, appeared in a medal of 1648.

A medal, designed in 1648 to commemorate the attempted release of King Charles I, contains the eye of God, with radiants emitted from the outside of an aureole of clouds. Within the motto is a five-pointed star:

The Latin motto ACUTUS EST ★ DEI OCULUS translates 'Piercing is the eye of God."

There is no suggestion that Charles I was himself a Mason, but the fact is that he was a personal friend of the Scottish Mason Sir Robert Moray, who (as we have seen in 44) had used the eye of Providence on his personal seal.

46. The eye of Providence appeared on American coinage at the end of the eighteenth century.

In 1785, two copper coins were minted in Vermont, the reverses of both of which displayed a central radiant eye on their reverses. There were twenty-six rays on each coin, thirteen of which were long ones, thirteen of which were punctuated by a six-rayed star:

This type of coin was popular for some time. For example, in 1783 a series of tokens was struck in Birmingham, England, for use in America. These were copper *Nova Constellatio* (New Constellation) coins, and were probably intended for use in New York.

47. The portrait of George Washington, at the center of the dollar bill, is highly symbolic.

It is entirely fitting that a portrait of Washington should appear on the front of the dollar bill. Although the great man seems to frown dourly at the world, it is a famous picture and one steeped in history.

The engraved portrait of George Washington on the face of the dollar bill is based on one of the several versions of the portrait painted by the American artist Gilbert Stuart in 1796. The original portrait was commissioned by Martha Washington, but Stuart never finished it, leaving the bottom part (Washington's clothing) untouched. Stuart made several finished copies of the painting, all of which he sold. The strange tension and swelling around the mouth is due to the fact that Washington had recently been fitted with a new set of false teeth. It is this, rather than any dour nature, which gives Washington's face such a tight-lipped expression.

This portrait of Washington dominates the dollar bill, and the face is deeply involved with the magical symbolism

of the design. For example, the oval is set in a linear structure that resembles the Greek letter omega:

Omega, Ω, was the final letter of the Greek alphabet,
which had been adopted by the early Christians as a symbol
of the end of things, or of the condition to which humanity
strives, in the future. In contrast, the first letter of the alphabet, the alpha, A, was adopted as a symbol of the beginning
of things—and, therefore, of the past.

Within this framework, the portrait of Washington is
symbolically linked with those future conditions, to which
the American nation strives. It is as though his portrait,
enclosed by the omega, is intended to suggest that
Washington's spirit is still guiding the destiny of the
American nation.

As we shall learn (49), the eye of Washington is at the
center of the dollar bill. This central placement reminds us
of the Constellatio Nova coin we examined in 25, in which
the eye is at the center of the stars representing the
American colonies. This placing of Washington's eye also
echoes the eye of Providence, which is at the center of the
triangle, above the pyramid of the dollar bill. The symbol-

ism is obvious: these associations are intended to suggest that Washington should be regarded symbolically as a kind of demigod. In spirit, he looks down over the destiny of the American nation, in much the same way as the eye of Providence overlooks the destiny of the world, from within the symbol of the Trinity.

48.There are *two* eyes, on either side of the dollar bill.

On the face of the bill are the two eyes of George Washington. On the back of the bill are the eye of Providence and the eye of the eagle.

If you fold a dollar bill along the top of the central ONE, the crease line will continue through the single eye above the pyramid.

The triangle △ containing the eye is exactly the same height as the star ✡ made up from the constellation of thirteen stars.

However, the two are not on the same horizontal level.

The graphic link between the two is the eye at the center of the triangle. If a horizontal line is drawn through the center of this eye, it touches the bottom radiant of the Star of David formed by the constellation of stars. This connecting line skims the top of the central word ONE. This could be a very subtle message.

The one eye, which completes the pyramid of thirteen levels, is united to the one star, which completes the bottom of the constellation of thirteen stars.

49. The right eye of George Washington is at the vertical center of the dollar bill.

If you fold the dollar bill vertically, you will find that the crease runs exactly through the right eye of George Washington.

The four figure ones [1] on this side of the note are so arranged as to center on the right eye of George Washington. With the aid of a straight edge, join together the diagonally opposite figures, from their topmost tips. You will find that the diagonals cross exactly over the right eye of George Washington. This tends to reinforce the symbolism we examined in 47.

The
WORD "AMERICA"

50. An historic map brought together the word "America" with the eagle.

The word "America" has attracted much sloppy attention in the literature devoted to magic. As a result, the origin of the word has been confused by many. In view of this, it is as well to set straight certain facts concerning this fascinating term.

The word was first used in a copy of a map of the world made in 1507. One irony of this extraordinary map is that, besides using for the first time the word "America," it traces parts of the coastline of the Americas and the discoverer after which the country had been named, Amerigo Vespucci. These facts are well known to historians. However, from our point of view, the most remarkable fact is that when this unique map was discovered in 1901, there was at the end of the book a fragment of a star map that included a detail of the constellation known as Lyra.

This is shown on the detail overleaf from the woodcut map made by Albrecht Dürer in 1515. This represented the celestial Eagle clutching to its body the Lyra, or Harp. Lyra is portrayed between Hercules (with the lion's skin over his left arm) and the bird (Avis), and above the swooping Eagle (Aquila). For ease of identification, Lyra has been reproduced alongside this detail of Dürer's star map.

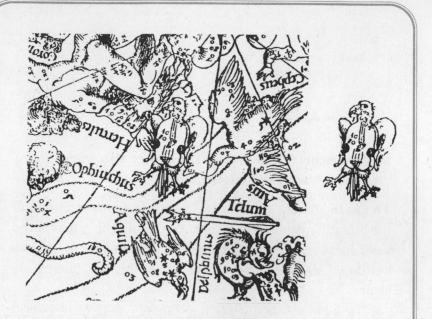

Remarkably, in 1820, this constellation, Lyra, caught the imagination of the Secretary of State, John Quincy Adams. He constructed from it a device for the passport of the United States of America, encircled by stars (see page 44).

51.The letter A is among the most magical of all letters.

The letter A is among the most magical of all letters. In numerology, it is equated with the number 1. This is true of all the first letters of alphabets used in the West today.

$$\text{Latin A} = 1$$
$$\text{Greek A (alpha)} = 1$$
$$\text{Hebrew } \aleph \text{ (aleph)} = 1$$

As we explore the symbolism of the dollar bill, we shall find that the letter A plays a most important role in its magical significance. This is not really surprising, in the present context, as we are dealing with a design intended for the ONE-dollar bill.

In the thirteenth-century sculpture below, Christ has an open book on his knee. The Latin words of this book translate as: *I am the End, I am the Beginning, the Creator of the Earth.* This symbolism is linked with the statement, made by Christ, that he would remain with Mankind until the end of time.

SVM
FINIS
SUM
PRINCI
PIUM

MAN
OIO:
CRE
ATOR

Many Christian works of art used the Greek letter A to represent the beginning and the final Greek letter, omega (which has the form ω), to represent the end. This explains why, in many medieval images of Christ, we find the letter

A on one side and the lowercase letter omega (ω) on the other. Together they represent the beginning and end. A good example (above) is a portrayal of Christ from the Roman catacombs of the fourth century A.D.

52. The letter A has always played an important role in magical symbolism.

Many medieval works on magic alert us to the hidden meaning of the letter A. In particular, the illustrations to the works of the seventeenth-century German mystic Jacob Boehme, make good use of the magical A.

Boehme linked this A with the eye of God. Partly, this was to reflect on the idea that God was the beginning of all things. However, there is another reason for this choice of letter. In Germany, the word for eye is *Auge*, and this begins with a letter A. God was not only the beginning; he was also the eye of the World.

The magical meaning of the detail from one of the Boehme works (page 71) is complex. What is of interest to us is the letter A towards the center of the design. This letter is inscribed within a letter O, which is the Roman equivalent of the Greek omega (ω). Thus, in this encircled A the beginning and the end meet. Past and future meet.

Above the encircled A is another magical design:

This consists of two triangles, side by side, one inverted. The one to the left is drawn with dotted lines, the one to the right, with continuous lines. In the center of each is an eye. Around the pair are flames. The one drawn with three lines is almost identical in form to the blazing triangle above the truncated pyramid of the dollar bill.

The eye in the latter triangle is almost like the crossbar of the letter A. This alerts us to one of the magical properties of the letter A. The letter A contains a triangle:

A Δ

Its form also suggests an incomplete pyramid:

From the point of view of magical symbolism, the letter A is a very powerful figure. It incorporates the idea of beginning, of the number 1, of unfinished work, of the eye of God, and of the Trinity.

Part of this significance is transferred to the word AMERICA, which begins and ends with the letter A, and which (from a magical point of view) hints at a hidden meaning in the word, linked with the meanings of the letters at the beginning and end of the word.

AMERICA

We see, then, that in terms of magical theory, the word AMERICA may be considered as the base of a triangle, the upper part of which is invisible. The word AMERICA is therefore a form of the truncated pyramid.

It may also be seen as the cross line of the A itself:

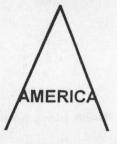

If we explore this idea in relation to the design of the dollar bill, we will discover some extraordinary secrets.

53.The symbolism of the A is part of the mystical significance of the dollar bill.

Strangely enough, something of the magical quality of the letter A is hinted at in the dollar bill. If you draw a line that follows the ascender of the letter A in the words ONE DOLLAR, at the bottom of the bill, you will find that this line passes exactly through the eye of the eagle.

If you turn the dollar bill over and draw a line through the descender of the letter A in the word STATES (above the portrait of George Washington), you will find that it continues into the descender of the letter A in the words ONE DOLLAR below the portrait.

This line passes through the left eye of George Washington.

54.The letter A of AMERICA plays an important role in the dollar bill.

The importance of the letter A, in the beginning and end the word AMERICA, was recognized by the designer of the dollar bill. It is easy to prove this for yourself with the aid of a ruler or straightedge.

If you place a straightedge on the ascender of the final A in AMERICA, above the eagle roundel, you will find that the line runs through the central star of the constellation:

If you place a straightedge on the descender of this same final A in AMERICA, you will find that the line runs through a white line on the engraved patterns of complex lines, above the bottom figure and letter ONE, towards the bottom of the note. This white line is exactly the same height at the descender of the letter A. It veers off, to touch the top of the figure 1.

If you place a straightedge on the ascender of the first A of AMERICA, you will find that the line continues onwards to cut the bottom line of the engraving precisely at the vertical center of the note.

If you place a straightedge on the descender of the first A of AMERICA, you will find that the line continues downwards to touch a distinctive white radiant in the pattern of the bill. This white radiant follows exactly the direction of this line and emerges from beneath the foliage at the bottom of the eagle roundel.

If you turn the note over, you will find that the A of AMERICA exhibits similar design characteristics on this side of the bill.

If you place a straightedge on the descender of the final A of AMERICA, you will find that this line continues *exactly* into the corner of the engraving. It is the boundary, suggested by this line, that accounts for the design of the olive leaves that fill the space marked by the line.

If you place a straightedge on the ascender of the final A of AMERICA, you will find that this cuts exactly into the chevron of the seal of the Department of the Treasury, cutting through the first of the thirteen stars. This chevron itself echoes the form of the A.

If you place a straightedge on the descender of this letter A, you will find that the line extends exactly through the bottom tip of the shield of the Treasury seal.

It seems evident that the descender and ascender of the first and last letters of AMERICA are an important element in the design of the note. The designer has used their angles to determine precisely where the seal of the Treasury should be located.

55. There are thirteen examples of the letter A on the front of the dollar bill.

On the front of the bill, the capital letter A appears thirteen times.

Reading downwards, these letters appear in the following words:

FEDERAL   1
STATES OF AMERICA   3

LEGAL   1
ALL AND PRIVATE   3
WASHINGTON, D.C.   1
DEPARTMENT TREASURY   2
DOLLAR   1
WASHINGTON   1
Total: 13

The
MOTTOES

56. The motto *E pluribus unum* is part of the magical numerology of the dollar bill.

The eagle of the dollar bill grasps in its beak a banderol, on which is written the Latin motto *E pluribus unum*, meaning "Out of many, the one."

Since the motto contains thirteen letters, the idea is that from the *thirteen* original colonies, there had grown the *one* United States.

Altogether, there are no fewer than ten examples of the number 13 on the dollar bill. As we proceed, we shall examine each of these occurrences.

There are six examples of the number 13 in the eagle roundel, as follows, three of which express the idea of "Out of many, the one."

The thirteen stars make ONE constellation.
The thirteen letters make ONE motto.
The thirteen leaves make ONE olive branch.
There are thirteen arrows.
There are thirteen vertical divisions on the shield.
There are thirteen horizontal divisions on the shield.

It is perhaps no accident that the division of the motto in this banderol results in the word *unum* being larger than the other two words. The Latin *unum* means one, and this is the ONE-dollar bill.

The angle of the word *unum* is such that it points up to the word ONE and the figure 1, which are crossed in the top right of the bill. This extended line crosses the bottom of the number 1 and just touches the bottom tip of the word ONE.

57. The Latin words ex *pluribus unum* are early Christian.

The Latin phrase *ex pluribus unum* is the more usual way of representing these three Latin words.

This phrase (which of course contains fourteen, rather than the all-important thirteen letters) is found in the autobiographical *Confessions* of the fifth-century Christian, Saint Augustine. The words are from a passage in which Augustine writes about friendship, which has (as he puts it) the power "to set ablaze our souls, and out of many make one." One presumes that the "many" are the many delights of friendship, and the "one" is love.

The Latin used by Augustine reads: *flagrare animos et ex pluribus unum facere*. It is interesting that Augustine uses a

Latin form that is technically more accurate than the Latin that appears on the dollar bill. Augustine wrote *ex pluribus*. However, if the words *ex pluribus unum* had be put on the Seal and dollar bill, the phrase would have contained fourteen letters, rather than the symbolically important thirteen.

58. The words *E Pluribus Unum* were first used as a motto by a French refugee, living in London.

The motto *E pluribus unum* is said to have been invented by a Protestant refugee from Rouen, with the appropriate name, Motteux. Pierre Antoine Motteux first published the motto in the January 1692 edition of *The Gentleman's Journal*. The detail below is from the title page of this edition:

The motto was almost certainly first sketched on proposed designs for the Great Seal by the Swiss artist Du Simitière, as may be seen in the tracing below:

It was probably first suggested by Thomas Jefferson, who was on the first committee set up by Congress to propose a design for the Seal.

59. The motto *Out of Many, the One* became very popular after the War of Independence.

After the War of Independence, the motto *E Pluribus Unum* appeared on a large number of early coins—for example, on the copper coins of 1787, minted for use in New Jersey and New York.

The motto expressed perfectly the sentiments of the Americans who were anxious to see a single nation forged from the sacrifices of the "many" states during the Revolutionary War.

60. The motto *Annuit Coeptis* is adapted from a prayer to the pagan gods.

Above the radiant triangle, and its eye of Providence, is the Latin motto *Annuit Coeptis*.

This motto has been taken from words written by the Roman poet Virgil in his epic *Aeneid*, where a prayer is made to Jupiter requesting aid in the daring enterprise ahead. The original words read, *Audacibus annue coeptis*, meaning "Favor our daring undertaking."

A similar line is also found in Virgil's *Georgics*, as a prayer to the gods for help. The Latin reads, *Da facilem cursum, atque audacibus annue coeptis* ("Give a smooth path, look kindly on my daring enterprise"). The Seal motto is a loose adaptation of one or other of the lines from Virgil. In either case, it is from a prayer invoking the pagan gods, who are implored to look with favor on the enterprise.

The adapted Latin, *Annuit Coeptis*, translates as "He favors our undertaking," and implies that the undertaking is a daring one.

Thus, in relation to the Seal and dollar bill, the motto petitions aid in the daring enterprise of completing the pyramid.

61. The motto *Novus Ordo Seclorum* was taken from a classical poem.

The Latin motto *Novus Ordo Seclorum*, below the truncated pyramid, means "A new order of the Ages." This motto was taken from a line by the poet Virgil, in one of his famous *Eclogues* that was interpreted by many as a prophecy of the coming of Christ:

Vltima Cumaei uenit iam carminis aetas; magnus ab integro seclorum nascitur ordo.

The original words read, *Magnus ab integro seclorum nascitur ordo*, meaning, "The great series of ages is born anew."

In 1780, Charles Thomson suggested that the motto should be used for the Great Seal. Thomson, then Secretary of Congress, believed that the civilization of America would eventually create a new world order. Perhaps the truncated pyramid was visualized as a symbol of America, which would be "completed" in some future period. As we have seen, the first letter of America, A, is a form that resembles both a pyramid and a truncated pyramid.

62. The Latin motto *Novus Ordo Seclorum* is in questionable Latin.

Properly speaking, the Latin should read *Novus Ordo Saeclorum*.

Vltima Cumaei uenit iam carminis aetas;
magnus ab integro saeclorum nascitur ordo.

However, the word did appear as both *saeclorum* and *seclorum* in various editions of Virgil, even though the former is generally preferred by scholars. We should bear in mind that if Thomson had written the word in the preferred way, then it would no longer consist of thirteen characters.

63. On the dollar bill, the motto *Novus Ordo Seclorum* is involved with a secret numerology.

Towards the end of the nineteenth century, Charles A. L. Totten had compared the pyramid on the Great Seal of America with the Great Pyramid of Gizeh in Egypt. He saw no objection to the thirteen courses on the Great Seal pyramid, since this number evidently symbolized the thirteen original colonies, which had faced up to Britain. However, he did make the surprising observation that this idea of thirteen was in close touch with the actual architecture of the Egyptian structure. (The pyramid roundel below is that drawn for Totten's book on the history of the Great Seal: we shall examine this design more fully on page 148).

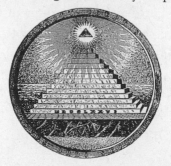

According to Totten, the original Great Pyramid had a number of courses that was a multiple of 13. The product of 17 x 13 was 221—the number of courses (including the capstone) of the Great Pyramid. The symbolism of the 13 was evident in the American design and required little comment. However, as Totten pointed out, the number 17 was also a factor of equal importance: the motto *Novus Ordo Seclorum* contained seventeen letters.

This numerology would have been of deep interest, had Totten not misread the number of courses on the pyramid. There were 211 original complete courses on the Great Pyramid, including the capstone.

In spite of Totten's error, the number 17 does play an important role in the symbolism of the Seal and the dollar bill.

Besides the seventeen letters of the motto, there are seventeen letters in the phrase OF THE UNITED STATES, which appears beneath the eagle roundel of the dollar bill.

When these seventeen characters of the motto are added to the nine characters of the Latin date, the sum is 26.

NOVUS ORDO SECLORUM 17

MDCCLXXVI 9

Divided by two, these give two groups of thirteen. This means that, when the thirteen-lettered motto on the pyramid roundel is taken into account, there are three groups of thirteen letters in that roundel:

NOVUS ORDO SECL 13

ORUM MDCCLXXVI 13

ANNUIT COEPTIS 13

64. There is only one motto in English on the dollar bill.

There are four mottoes on the dollar bill, only one of which is in English. This is the motto, *In God We Trust*, above the central ONE.

IN GOD WE TRUST

Like the three Latin mottoes, this is carved over one of the doorways leading into the Senate Chamber of the Capitol Building in Washington, D.C. It is carved over the South entrance to the Senate Chamber. *Annuit Coeptis* is carved over the east entrance doorway. *Novus Ordo Seclorum* is carved over the west entrance doorway.

In magic, these orientations to south, west, and east have a deep significance related to the position of the Sun. In the engraving on page 90, we see the full sun of midday (Midi) at the top, which means that the triangle at the center of the design is resting on its base. The seven-pointed star symbolizes the seven planets, and the seven letters around the star spell out UNIVERS—the French for "universe."

As the diagram indicates, when the Sun is at its highest point (and therefore at its most powerful), it is to the south. This suggests that the English motto, *In God We Trust*, is regarded as being the most powerful or important of the four official mottoes we have examined.

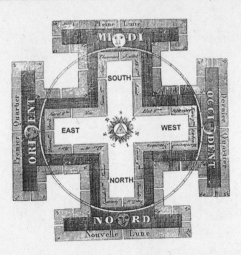

This importance is confirmed by the fact that, in 1962, the three stars on the back of the Speaker's rostrum were replaced by the motto, *In God We Trust*. The House Chamber lies to the south of the Senate chamber: this suggests that the motto is designed to link together the two houses through trust in God.

In the magical tradition, the east, which is the place of sunrise, where the light of day first becomes visible, marks the beginning of things. It rules over new impulses. This corresponds with the nature of the motto, *Annuit Coeptis*, which implies that God has favored the beginning of the new enterprise of building a new civilization.

The west, or occident, is linked in the magical tradition with the end of things—that is, with the ultimate aim or purpose behind things. The position of the motto *Novus Ordo Seclorum* suggests that the new order is itself the aim and purpose of the American civilization.

The Latin *E Pluribus Unum* is carved within a panel behind the Vice-President's rostrum.

The
PYRAMID

65. The truncated pyramid consists of thirteen courses.

The United States had been founded in 1776, by an agreement undertaken by the thirteen colonies. It is, therefore, hardly surprising that the pyramid should be represented by the designers of the Great Seal as having thirteen completed courses.

The Latin date is marked on the bottom course: this implies that the building of the pyramid was begun in 1776. There is no indication as to when it will be finished.

66. The idea of a truncated pyramid was Masonic.

Francis Hopkinson, who designed the pyramid for the fifty-dollar bill for the Continental currency (page 94), was almost certainly a Mason.

There may be little doubt that it was this truncated pyramid, with its thirteen courses, that suggested to Barton the idea for a pyramid on the reverse of the Seal.

It is possible that Hopkinson's currency design for the fifty-dollar bill also had an influence on the use of the eye in the Great Seal. This currency contained the image of an eye within a cloud of glory.

67. The source of the truncated pyramid on the first Seal proposal.

The first drawing of a truncated pyramid for the Seal proposal was that made by William Barton, in 1782. This is a stepped pyramid of thirteen courses. Its proportions appear to have been copied from a work on the Great Pyramid by an English professor at Oxford University, John Greaves.

Below (left) is Barton's pyramid. This is compared, with a section from Greaves's engraving of the Great Pyramid, which he used to illustrated his book on the subject (right).

Greaves had traveled to Gizeh, and had studied the Great Pyramid in great detail. The proportion of his design was very accurate, even though it did not represent all of the 202 remaining courses in the historic pyramid (see entire engraving, on next page).

It is, of course, the truncated top that is of interest to us here. It had also interested Greaves, who wrote, in a spelling so representative of the eighteenth century, that the great structure

ends not in a point, as Mathematicall Pyramids doe, but in a litle flat, or square . . . 9 feet in bredth at the top.

The outside of the first Pyramid

Barton's drawing rightly emphasized this truncation, which is an important part of his symbolism. He was anxious to portray a pyramid that was yet to be completed. In contrast, Greaves had been interested in the fact that the pyramid had once been completed, but had been destroyed, by time and man, both at the top and along the four faces.

Although seven of the top courses are now missing or are fragmentary, so massive is the pyramid itself that the loss is scarcely noticeable from the ground. Even so, the Arabs who helped destroy the Great Pyramid (by defacing it of its white marble to build their holy buildings in Cairo) claimed that the platform was large enough for eleven camels to lie down on. Greaves, with less imagination, had counted nine "massy stones" on the platform, besides "two that are wanting at the angles."

The surviving nine seem to have worked their way into the first dollar-bill proposal. Although Barton's sketch does not represent the stones in the staggered sequence of the Great Pyramid masonry, his choice of three stones for the top suggests that he visualized the top as consisting of nine stones (that is, 3 x 3 = 9).

68. The unfinished pyramid appeared in art long before the eighteenth century.

The image of an unfinished pyramid appeared in a number of devices and medals long before it was adopted by the American revolutionaries. In most cases, the symbolism of the truncated pyramid seems to have suggested the idea of "work unfinished."

For example, Pope Adrian VI, who reigned for only one year, from 1522 to 1523, adopted as his papal device a pyramid in the process of being built. The motto attached to the device read *Ut ipse finiam*, meaning, "In order that I might finish it personally." Adrian appears to have visualized the pyramid as being a symbol of the living church, which he would like to help towards completion.

In an engraving of 1743, a female personification of Art is shown being presented to Great Nature (see page 98). In the background is a steep unfinished pyramid. Perhaps this is a reference to the idea that Art itself is an activity without end.

69. The pyramid was a symbol of stability and virtue.

The pyramid figures as a symbol of stability in a number of emblem books of the seventeenth century. The one opposite is from an emblem book of 1635.

This emblem is a curious one. The roundel portrays a flying pyramid, even though the text expounds upon the stability of "a true triangled Pyramide," which stands fast against winds and raging seas. The moral is that human virtue should aspire to the same stability that the pyramid offers. The writer of the text prays to God that he may be granted this security in the raging seas of his own inner life:

> But, fixe thou so, this weake desire of mine,
> Upon the *Vertues* of thy *Rocke* divine,
> That I, and that invaluable *Stone*,
> May bee incorporated into *One*:
> And, then, it will bee neither shame, nor pride,
> To say, my *Vertues*, will unmov'd abide.

Within such a context, the truncated pyramid (that invaluable *Stone*) is a symbol of virtue as yet incomplete.

70. The number of individual stones in the pyramid is magical.

As we know, the pyramid consists of thirteen courses, and this symbolism was intended to refer to the original thirteen colonies.

In 1928, the American symbolist Manly P. Hall attempted to show that there were seventy-two stones in the pyramid, exclusive of the block that contains the Latin date. This exciting idea began to circulate widely among those interested in the secret symbolism of the Seal. The excitement was quite reasonable because the number 72 is one of the most sacred of all magical numbers.

It is surprising that Manly Hall's notion was so widely accepted. The picture of the pyramid roundel (from the seal of 1904), which he reproduced to support his idea, does not have seventy-two stones. It actually has seventy-three, excluding the block containing the date.

It seems that Manly Hall did not count the stones with sufficient care.

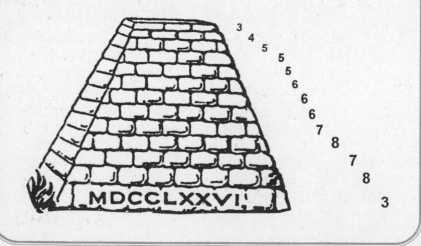

However, this thesis of Manly Hall did influence the later design of the dollar bill.

Even with the aid of a powerful magnifying glass, it is far from easy to count the stones on the dollar-bill pyramid. The difficulty is that the engraver has used vertical lines for shading, and these are not always easy to distinguish from the vertical mortar lines.

However, a serious attempt to count these stones convinces one that the designer, Edward M. Weeks, had been influenced by Manly Hall's numerology. Weeks's own pyramid on the dollar bill is represented with the lowest block in the form of a single monolith. This gives a total of seventy-two blocks in the face of the structure.

This number 72 is one of the most sacred numbers in all magical systems. For example, it is believed that there are seventy-two ways of writing and pronouncing the name of God.

The engraving on the following page, from a seventeenth-century book dealing with magical symbolism, gives these seventy-two names, along with their many associations.

The number 72 is also linked with the movement of the Sun. Due to a phenomenon called precession, the Sun appears to fall back against the stars. This rate of precession is one degree every seventy-two years.

71. The pyramid on the dollar bill is a magical symbol.

The number 72, which we find on the pyramid, appears in one of the most important of all magical symbols. This figure is called the *tetractys* and consists of the four letters of the Hebrew name of God, arranged in four lines:

In the cabbalistic system (that is, in the secret wisdom of the Hebrews), each letter of the alphabet is accorded a number. The letter ' (yod) is given the number 10. The letter ה (heh) is given the number 5. The letter ו (vav) is given the number 6. It follows that these numerical equivalents may be substituted for the letters in the *tetractys*, as follows:

10

5 10

6 5 10

5 6 5 10

Added together, they give a total of 72, which is the sacred number of the names of God, and the number of stones in the face of the dollar-bill pyramid:

10

[5 + 10] = 15

[6 + 5 + 10] = 21

[5 + 6 + 5 + 10] = 26

TOTAL = 72

The magical figure of the *tetractys* is clearly linked with the pyramid of the dollar bill. There is one other magical *tetractys*, from the seventeenth century, which forms an even closer link with the pyramid.

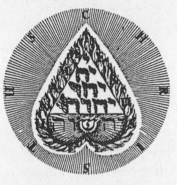

This *tetractys* (above) is set within a flaming triangle, which has the outer form of a heart. The radiant triangle above the truncated pyramid may be seen as a reference to this burning *tetractys*.

In the magical tradition, this burning triangle of the *tetractys* is linked with the three persons of the Trinity. The name of Christ is spelled around the radiant [CHRISTUS]. The name of God the Father [Jehovah] is spelled out at the foot of the triangle, in Hebrew [יהוה], and the symbol of Spirit is given in the middle of this latter word, in the Hebrew letter *shin*: שׁ

Here, then, the Trinity is represented in the form of a radiant, or burning, triangle. It seems highly likely that the radiant triangle that completes the pyramid is itself a reference to symbolism of this order.

72. Was a reverse of the Seal, with the truncated pyramid, cut in 1885?

The truncated pyramid has always been something of a mystery. In 1782, Congress had ordered that the die for this reverse of the Seal should be cut. However, so far as it is possible to tell, it never was cut.

It is possible that when Tiffany & Company cut the obverse of the die in 1885, they also cut a die for the reverse of the Seal. A sketch for this reverse had been submitted by Tiffany, and at the end of the work, the company billed for both the obverse and the reverse. The drawing follows that we examined on page 85, save for three important differences. In his sketch, the Tiffany designer misspelled the word *Coeptis*, representing it as *Coeptus*. Aware of the importance of the number 13, he made an effort to place the radiant triangle within a sunburst of that number of radiants:

He completely ignored the numerical significance of the pyramid. Whoever made this sketch represented the pyramid with 126 stones.

Whether the die was actually cut remains a mystery. A newspaper reporter from the *Daily Graphic* visited the Tiffany workshop in 1885, while the die was being cut. In his account of the visit, he mentioned that there was no trace of a die for the pyramid reverse.

The surviving official records are full of inconsistencies. From these it does seem that the Department of State was anticipating that Tiffany would provide a reverse die.

However, if the die was supplied, it was never used, and its present whereabouts are unknown.

73. The first official use of the pyramid image.

In 1882, a Centennial Medal, designed to commemorate the first one hundred years of the Great Seal, was minted. Surprisingly, the designs for this medal deviated enormously from those used for the Great Seal. On the obverse was a version of the eagle, in which the constellation of stars was dispersed, rather than being arranged in a stellar pattern above the head of the eagle.

On the reverse was a version of the pyramid—the first time the pyramid had appeared in official use. However, this was not the pyramid one finds on the Seal or dollar bill. It is a stepped pyramid, without any indications of stones. It is also designed to represent the east face of the pyramid (the north face is just visible to the left of the medal).

Although intended to commemorate the centennial of the Great Seal, this pyramid, with its extensive radiants above the truncation and the two mottoes, was *not* based on the Seal pyramid. It was copied, detail for detail, from an image that has the reputation of being the first engraved image of the reverse of the Great Seal (below).

This engraving appeared in an issue of the *Columbian Magazine* in 1786. The only significant deviation made from the print of 1786 was the addition of the dates, 1782–1882, on either side of the pyramid. Rather than commemorating the design of the Great Seal, the medal seemed to commemorate the *Columbian Magazine* design.

74. The pyramid now on the dollar bill was once the subject of a presidential address.

On October 9, 1899, President McKinley delivered a speech in Chicago, the general theme of which was based on the Great Seal of the United States. He chose to emphasize the close relationship between the pyramid on the Great Seal and the United States.

> Has the pyramid lost any of its strength? The pyramid put on the reverse side of the great seal of the United States by the fathers as signifying strength and duration, has it lost any of its strength? [Voices, "No!"] Has the republic lost any of its virility? Has the self-governing principle been weakened? Is there any present menace to our stability and duration? [Voices, "No!"] These questions bring but one answer. The republic is sturdier and stronger than ever before. [Great applause.] . . .
>
> After one hundred and twenty-three years the pyramid stands unshaken. It has had some severe shocks, but it remains immovable. It has endured the storms of war, only to be strengthened. It stands firmer and gives greater promise of duration than when the fathers made it the symbol of their faith. [Applause.]

President McKinley was a Mason.

MAGIC NUMBERS

75. The date MDCCLXXVI is part of the magical numerology of the dollar bill.

Charles Thomson, the Secretary of Congress, first proposed in 1780 that the Latin date should be used on the Great Seal.

MDCCLXXVI

Thomson appears to have been aware of some hidden meaning within the date. As we shall see, the designer of the dollar bill, Edward M. Weeks, made extensive and creative use of the hidden meaning.

The Latin date at the base of the pyramid is the equivalent of 1776. The Latin consists of nine characters—the same as the numbers of letters in ONE DOLLAR.

The large ONE in the center of the bill is built up from nine shaded units.

In all, there are nine words (including the Latin date) in the two roundels. The eagle's tail consists of nine feathers.

76. When the Roman date on the pyramid is translated into Arabic numerals (1776), a remarkable numerology is revealed.

In numerology, the 1776 may be seen as:

$$[(1 + 6 = 7) 7 \text{ and } 7]$$

This is three sevens, or 777—a combination of the two most magical of all numbers—the 3 and the 7. In this case, it is the number 7 repeated three times.

The numbers 3 and 7 appear on the dollar bill on several occasions. For example, the two mottos, *Novus ordo Seclorum* and *E pluribus unum*, consist of three words. The inscription, THE GREAT SEAL, below the pyramid roundel, also consists of three words: this is completed by the words OF THE UNITED STATES below the eagle seal, to make seven words in total.

The words at the top and bottom of this side of the dollar bill also consist of seven words: THE UNITED STATES OF AMERICA and ONE DOLLAR.

On this face of the bill, the word ONE is repeated seven times—that is, if we include the word *unum* (which means "one") from the motto *E pluribus unum*.

The number 1776 adds up to 21 $(1 + 7 + 7 + 6 = 21)$. This number, 21, is another example of three and seven—in this case, $3 \times 7 = 21$. There are twenty-one words in the middle of the dollar bill (reading from left to right):

ANNUIT CŒPTIS
MCCLXXVI
NOVUS ORDO SECLORUM
THE GREAT SEAL
IN GOD WE TRUST
ONE
E PLURIBUS UNUM
OF THE UNITED STATES.

77. The mystical numbers 3 and 7, and their product, 21, play an important role in the design of the dollar bill.

The English words on the back of the dollar bill have been designed to reflect each number from one to seven. This is the analysis:

1. ONE
2. ONE DOLLAR
3. THE GREAT SEAL
4. IN GOD WE TRUST
5. THE UNITED STATES OF AMERICA
6. ONE (REPEATED SIX TIMES)
7. THE GREAT SEAL OF THE UNITED STATES

The Latin words and numbers on the back of the dollar bill have been designed to reflect the numbers from 1 to 3.

1. MDCCLXXVI
2. ANNUIT COEPTIS
3. NOVUS ORDO SECLORUM

Three times seven (3 x 7) is, of course, 21.

78. The mystical 21 plays an important role in the design of the dollar bill.

On the back of the dollar bill, and at the very bottom, are the words ONE DOLLAR. The broad letters of these two words are shaded. In all, there are twenty-one areas of shading in the nine letters.

The nine letters are built up from twenty-one distinct units (the bowl and the descending flourish of the final letter, R, is cunningly designed to be read as a single form).

At the top of the front of the dollar bill are the three words FEDERAL RESERVE NOTE. At the bottom are the words ONE DOLLAR, over which is the name WASHINGTON. Altogether, these words contain thirty-seven characters. In numerology, this is 3 x 7, which is 21.

The letters USA appear on the back of the dollar bill twenty-six times. The letter U appears nine times, the letter S appears nine times, and the letter A appears eight times.

79. The words at the top and bottom of the reverse of the dollar bill point to a sacred number.

The words THE UNITED STATES OF AMERICA at the top of both sides of the bill, and ONE DOLLAR at the bottom of both sides, total thirty-three characters. This is regarded as a sacred number.

The central phrase IN GOD WE TRUST and the large ONE below this have been designed to reflect this number,

33, because Jesus Christ lived on earth for that number of years. As we have seen, the ONE consists of nine units. To give a three-dimensional quality to the ONE, the designer has placed behind these units eleven shadows.

This means that the ONE consists of twenty units, in all. To this we add the number ONE [1] itself, to give 21. If we add to this the twelve letters of IN GOD WE TRUST, we have a total of 33.

All told, there are thirty-three words or groups of numbers on the back of the dollar bill. What is usually missed in a count is the number below the end of the large central ONE.

80. The shield on the dollar bill has two sets of thirteen stripes.

The shield on the dollar bill has thirteen vertical stripes, alternating white with black. The central vertical, which is the longest, is white.

The horizontal bar on the shield is "colored" by thirteen horizontal lines. (In heraldry, there is a strict convention whereby line, dots, and so on represent colors.)

Hopkinson proposed the idea for a shield with thirteen stripes. This was the same Hopkinson who had designed the flag of the United States in 1777.

Hopkinson's first design for the Seal consisted of thirteen diagonal stripes, alternating white and red. It was William Barton who proposed that these stripes should become horizontal. Surprisingly, those responsible for the design of the Seal did not immediately adopt this suggestion. Thomson later proposed that they should be represented not as horizontal stripes but as chevrons. Later, Barton returned to the idea of vertical stripes.

81. The olive branch on the dollar bill has thirteen leaves.

The olive branch in the eagle roundel of the dollar bill has thirteen leaves and thirteen olives. This is certainly intended to symbolize the peaceful intentions of the United States.

However, it was only with the Seal design of 1890 that the olive was finally represented as having thirteen leaves. The olive branch of 1782 had sixteen leaves; that of 1841 had seventeen. That the Seal of 1890 should have adopted the thirteen originally intended for the first design was probably due to the insistence of Totten, whose efforts had led to the minting of the commemorative medal of 1882 (see p. 106).

In fact, as Charles A. L. Totten had recognized, shortly after the end of the War of Independence, the symbolism of the thirteen-leaved olive branch seems to have become an important part of American symbolism. The coin of 1791 (above) represents George Washington as the first President. The eagle on the obverse grasps an olive branch with thirteen leaves and a sheaf of thirteen arrows.

While this symbolism of thirteen caught the spirit of the age, not all coinage design made use of it. For example, another Washington one-cent piece, minted in the same year, depicted the eagle grasping an olive branch with only eight leaves and six arrows (see page 117). Around the head of the eagle are eight five-pointed stars.

82. The word ONE and the figure I appear ten times on the reverse of the dollar bill.

The word ONE and the figure 1 appear ten times on the reverse of the dollar bill. The ten emerge from the following sources:

Number 1 repeated four times in each corner:	4
The word ONE repeated four times in each corner:	4
The word ONE inbetween the two roundels:	1
The word ONE in ONE DOLLAR at bottom of note:	1

The word WASHINGTON, beneath the portrait, consists of ten letters.

In numerology, the figure 10 may be reduced (by addition) to 1 + 0 = 1. It is the only binary that may be so reduced. This means, therefore, that 10 is the numerical equivalent, which offers an example of "one may obtain 'one out of the many'" (*E pluribus unum*).

In view of this numerology, we may feel disappointed that the large ONE, which runs between the two roundels of the dollar bill, consists of nine distinct elements.

This appears to have nothing to do with the magical 10 that reduces to 1. However, behind the word ONE is a shadow. This shadow consists of eleven units.

If you add the 11 (shadow) to the 9 of the ONE, you obtain 20. Divide by the two different forms, and you obtain 10. The ONE and its shadow conspire together to make 10, which is the magical 1.

It may be argued that we dealt with the ONE and its shadow in 79, and came to a different numerological conclusion. However, in magic, it is permissible to regard all symbols as containing several levels of meaning. Magical symbols may be approached in a multitude of different ways.

83. The word ONE and the figure I appear seven times on the front of the dollar bill.

The word ONE and the figure 1 appear seven times on the face of the dollar bill. In making this count, one must ignore the ephemeral numbers that vary from series to series (see page xii). The seven emerge from the following sources:

Number 1 repeated four times in each corner........................4

The word ONE in ONE DOLLAR at bottom of note 1

The word ONE to left of George Washington,
      overprinted by Department of the Treasury stamp........1

The figure 1 in the date, 1789, on the
      Department of the Treasury stamp................................1

TOTAL 7

The word ONE and the figure 1 appear ten times on the back of the dollar bill. The ten emerge from the following sources:

The number 1 is crossed by the word ONE in each
      of the four corners 8

The word ONE in the center of the note 1

The word ONE in ONE DOLLAR at bottom of note 1

TOTAL..10

On the back of the note, there is the Roman I, on the base of the pyramid, and the word *unum* (one) in the motto of the eagle roundel. The total from both sides of the dollar bill is therefore $7 + 10 + 2 = 19$.

In numerology, 19 may be reduced to 10 $(1 + 9 = 10)$, which in turn reduces to the magical 1.

84. The five words in the center of the dollar bill could be designed to be read together.

In the center of the dollar bill is the word ONE. Above this appears the national motto, IN GOD WE TRUST.

Since the phrase IN GOD WE TRUST has twelve letters, it is possible to think of the ONE in terms of its numerical equivalent, which is 1. If we do this, then the five words give a magical total of thirteen letters.

Since these five words are united by this numerology, the implication is they may be read as: IN *ONE* GOD WE TRUST.

85. The reverse of the dollar bill contains thirteen examples of the number 13.

It is well known that the number 13 dominates in the design of the dollar bill. What is not so well known, however, is that there are thirteen examples of the number 13 on the reverse of the dollar bill.

The following examples of 13 have already been examined:

On the reverse of the bill:

[1] The number of letters in the motto, *Annuit Cœptis.*

[2] & [3] The number of letters in the motto *Novus Ordo Seclorum* and the Latin date MDCCLXXVI.

[4] The number of letters in the motto *E pluribus unum.*

[5] The thirteen levels of the pyramid.

[6] The thirteen stars in the constellation above the eagle.

[7] The thirteen horizontal lines on the band at the top of the shield.

[8] The thirteen vertical stripes on the shield.

[9] The thirteen olive leaves.

[10] The thirteen berries on the olive leaves.

[11] The thirteen arrows.

What is not so widely known is that:

[12] & [13] On the reverse of the bill, there are decorative leaves to the left of the pyramid roundel and to the right of the eagle roundel. The decorative spines of these leaves each consists of thirteen nodules:

THE EAGLE

86. The eagle is an ancient symbol of spiritual power.

From very ancient times, the eagle has been a symbol of spiritual power. Among the ancient Romans, it was the bird of Jupiter, the chief of the gods.

From the very earliest days of astronomy, it had been a star-bird, formed from the constellations to the west of the Dolphin, flying across the Milky Way (above). This was supposed to represent Jupiter himself, though in some early star lists it is called merely "Jupiter's bird." Given the graphic importance attached to the eye of the eagle (see

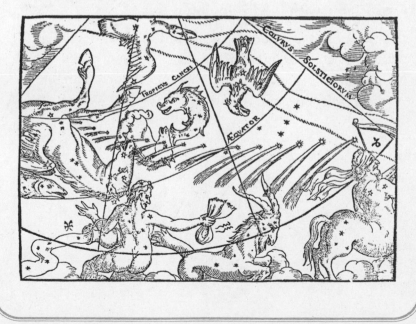

page 74), it is interesting to learn that the astronomers of the Euphrates called it the Living Eye. In the medieval woodcut on page 125, which illustrates the passage of the Great Comet of 1577 across the skies, the large star on the eagle's breast represents the pale yellow star, Altair.

In early Christian time, the eagle appeared in art and architecture as a symbol of the new "chief among the gods," Christ. In the Cloisters Collection, in the Metropolitan Museum of Art, New York, there is a silver chalice of the fifth century that shows Christ seated above an eagle that has outstretched wings.

In later times, the image of the eagle was adopted as a symbol of material power—it became the bird of kings, emperors, and princes.

87. In medieval art and symbolism, the eagle was associated with the five-pointed star.

In the medieval period, the eagle was regarded as a magical figure. A good example of this may be seen in the detail from the notebooks of the thirteenth-century architect, Villard de Honnecourt, below:

Villard de Honnecourt traced in the heraldic image of a displayed eagle the form of the five-pointed star, or pentagram. This meant that the eagle was viewed as being the equivalent of the five-pointed star—in terms of both symbolism and numerology.

This union of symbol and number was of profound importance to medieval architects and artists, for whom Honnecourt made these drawings. This association with the number 5 may explain why, in the fifteenth century, Maximilian I adopted the image of an eagle with a five-lettered motto: *Aquila electa Jovis omnia vincit* ("the eagle, chosen by Jupiter, conquers all things"). Similarly, in the sixteenth century, the alchemist-emperor, Rudolph II of Bohemia and Hungary, adopted the image of an eagle holding a dart, with the enigmatic motto of five letters, A.D.S.I.T., the meaning of which is uncertain.

88. Originally, the bald-headed eagle on the Seal was intended to represent Congress.

In his proposal for the design of the Seal, submitted in 1782, William Barton (amending proposals made by Charles Thomson, the Secretary of State) specified that the eagle, bearing the shield on its breast, should be "an American [bald-headed] Eagle."

Thomson's earlier proposal (which was eventually adopted) had insisted that the left talon of the bird should grasp thirteen arrows. However, he did not specify how many leaves should be on the olive branch. As we have seen, this has been rectified on the dollar bill. The olive branch on the dollar bill not only has thirteen leaves, but also contains thirteen olive berries.

William Barton had explained the symbolism of the Eagle very clearly. He had written that "the Eagle displayed is the Symbol of the supreme Power & Authority, and signifies the Congress." This explanation was sensible, for it was Congress that had control over the policies leading to either peace (the olive branch) or war (the arrows).

Although the intended symbolism of the eagle was clear from the very beginning—that it represented Congress—this was quickly forgotten. Within less than a decade, it was widely believed that the eagle was intended as a symbol of empire.

89. In magical symbolism, the eagle is the attribute of the highest God.

The eagle was one of the old symbols for empire. According to Colonna, whose work on Egyptian hieroglyphs deeply influenced Renaissance art, the eagle with outstretched wings signified "empire."

The eagle is one of the five symbols of the five senses. Because the eagle was fabled for its keen eyesight, it was chosen to represent the sense of sight.

In ancient Greek and Roman mythology, the eagle was the attribute of the god Zeus, or Jupiter, who is seated to the left in the woodcut, below.

The connection between Jupiter and the eagle is especially interesting in light of the motto above the truncated pyramid. As we have seen, *Annuit Coeptis* was derived from a prayer to the pagan god Jupiter, seeking his support for the enterprise ahead.

Held in the beak of Jupiter's bird, in the eagle roundel, is a symbol of this "daring enterprise"—the forging of one out of many.

The two thirteen-letter mottoes seem to form the link between the two roundels. In fact, this link is more than merely verbal, or numerical. If you were to superimpose the eagle roundel over the pyramid roundel, you would find that the tips of the eagle's wings are so located as to act as supports for the pyramid motto, *Annuit Coeptis*.

The right wing tip runs exactly through the apex of the all-important first letter, A. The left runs through the center of the final letter, S.

90. The dollar-bill roundels were designed in such a way as to be considered together as a single magical figure.

The superimposition of the eagle on the pyramid roundel leads us to a most amazing magical device hidden in the dollar bill.

In the alchemical tradition, the four elements (which were believed to lie behind all matter) were symbolized as triangles.

The triangle resting on its base represents Fire: △
The triangle resting on its apex represents Water: ▽

That with a horizontal line, resting on its base, represents
Air: △

That with a horizontal line, resting on its apex,
represents Earth: ▽

In the magical tradition, these four symbols were com-
bined to make the single star, or Seal of Solomon,
which we have already examined: ✡

The alchemical engraving below gives these four symbols:

The basic structures of the two roundels were designed
to represent two triangles. The pyramid roundel clearly contains a triangle resting on its base:

The eagle roundel contains a triangle resting on its apex.

Given the radiant eye above the pyramid, we may reasonably assume that the pyramid triangle represents Fire. Given that the eagle is a bird, we may assume that the eagle triangle represents Air. This is a happy combination: the oxygen of air feeds the flames of fire, and the resultant flames stream upwards, towards the heavens.

This symbol of aspiration is beautifully set out in the superimposition we have just examined. The apex of the triangle slips exactly into the triangle of stars in the constellation. The lower rotundity of the eye completes this "circle" made by the stars. The masonry of the pyramid seems to be lifted upwards by the two wings that sprout from its sides. Each end of the base of the pyramid touches the talons and seems to be lifted into the air by these.

If anyone has any doubts that the design of the dollar bill is rooted in magical symbolism, they need only examine this strange yet meaningful figure.

91. The order of the eagle and pyramid roundels on the dollar bill was determined by President Roosevelt.

Before President Franklin D. Roosevelt approved the design for the dollar bill in 1935, he found it necessary to amend it. In the original design, the pyramid roundel was on the right, the eagle roundel on the left. In his instructions to the

designer and engravers to change the order of the roundels, he represented the pyramid by means of a triangle and the eagle in a form that would fit into an inverted triangle.

Roosevelt wanted to place beneath them the two blocks of wording that now appear on the dollar bill:

THE GREAT SEAL   OF THE UNITED STATES

Evidently, he felt that the latter phrase should fall under the eagle rather than under the pyramid. It seemed more appropriate to associate the United States with the eagle than with the pyramid. Perhaps Roosevelt was not aware of the fact, yet he was returning to the symbolism first proposed by William Barton in 1782. As we have seen, Barton visualized the bald-headed eagle as the symbol of Congress—in which the entire political might of the United States is vested.

The amended design, with Roosevelt's initialed approval, is still preserved in the Bureau of Engraving and Printing.

92. There were *three* birds in the earliest designs of the Great Seal of America.

In the early designs for the Seal, drawn by William Barton, in 1782, there were three birds. The first of his designs (which has survived only in a written form, or blazon) included a cock as the crest. This was intended to symbolize "Vigilance & Fortitude"—which were viewed as "two most excellent Qualities, Necessary in a free Country."

On the shield was a white eagle with wings outstretched, on top of a column. This bird was proposed as being "emblematical of the Sovereignty of the Government of the United States." At the top of the American flag, held by one of the two supporters of the shield, was the dove of peace. The female holding up this flag was a personification of the United States, or, as Barton put it, "the Genius of the American confederated Republic."

In the second design by William Barton (which was also drawn in 1782, and has survived in a colored painting), there were still *three* birds. However, these were not altogether the same as those in the earlier design.

The cock had been changed to a silver eagle. In its right talon, it held a golden sword, on which hung a laurel wreath. In its left was the flag of the United States.

The eagle, which had stood upon the pillar of the first design, was now changed into a phoenix, sitting in a nest of flames (below). We shall examine this symbol shortly.

The dove remained in the right hand of the female personification of the United States.

93. It has been suggested that the original eagle of the Great Seal was really a phoenix.

The original seal depicted a crested eagle. As the two details below indicate, this eagle was very different from the one that now appears on the Seal and on the dollar bill.

In 1928, the scholar Manley Palmer Hall suggested that the crested eagle was intended to be a phoenix. His evidence was an engraving of an Egyptian version of the phoenix that had a headdress with a crest upon it (see below), similar to that on the head of the first eagle on the Great Seal.

This Egyptian picture showed a winged god kneeling as though in prayer, with a five-pointed star below his uplifted arms.

Manley Hall had taken this image from the first edition of a book by the English Egyptologist Sir J. Gardner Wilkinson. What Manley Hall failed to realize was that, in a later edition of the book (printed in 1878), Wilkinson had admitted that he had made a mistake, and the phoenix-man did not represent the phoenix at all. Instead, it represented "the pure soul of the ruler."

Another thing that Manly Hall failed to recognize was that it was commonplace for eagles in heraldry and in emblem books to have crests. An example is in the drawing of an emblematic eagle below. This eagle, grasping an imperial sword and olive branches, represents "peace and war."

94. A phoenix, in flames, was proposed for the original Great Seal, as a symbol of a renewed liberty.

In 1782, William Barton proposed a phoenix as part of his own design for the Great Seal.

In his description of the Seal, Barton proposed that the arms should include a golden pillar of the Doric order. On top of this was to stand a phoenix in flames, with wings expanded. A sketch of this detail of Barton's proposal is given below.

In proposing the phoenix, Barton intended it to refer to ancient mythology. In this mythology, at the end of each period (some say, this is a five-hundred-year span, while others say it is a period of eight hundred years) the phoenix would set itself alight, and be consumed. Then, from the ashes, the same bird would be renewed, to live again, in an endless cycle of birth and death.

Barton saw the burning phoenix of his Seal design as being "emblematic of the expiring Liberty of Britain, revived by her Descendants, in America."

95. It is possible that the bald-headed eagle had its origins in European heraldry.

It has been proposed by historians that the eagle, first proposed by William Barton for the Seal, was derived from a book on heraldry. This book, which was owned by Benjamin

Franklin, had been printed in 1597. The design of this eagle is reproduced below:

To the right of the eagle is a bundle of lightning, which is usually associated with the pagan god Jupiter. To the right is an olive branch.

The eagle finally adopted for the Seal and dollar bill clutches in its right talon a similar olive branch. The branch in the design of 1597 had seventeen olive leaves. The one adopted for the Seal has thirteen leaves.

The eagle of the dollar bill does not grasp forks of lightning or thunderbolts associated with Jupiter, but a bundle of arrows. The symbolism of the arrows points to projectiles—instruments of war—that may be directed by man rather than by a God.

As a matter of fact, the eagle was widely used in alchemy. In certain texts, the crowned eagle was seen as a symbol of a successfully completed stage in the search for the manufacture of the secret Philosopher's Stone, which could confer long life and incredible riches (see over).

Perhaps such symbolism permits us to view the eagle of the dollar bill as a reference to fulfillment and achievement in the past. In this respect, it is being contrasted with the achievement of the future—that involved with the completing of the pyramid.

96. The hidden symbolism of the arrows.

In the popular view, the olive branch and arrows in the talons of the eagle represent peace and war. However, the symbolism seems to be more subtle than that.

From the early records of proposals as to the form the Seal should take, we are led to the opinion that the arrows were not intended to represent merely a warlike impulse. Thomas Jefferson had argued that a proper device for the American states would be the image of a father presenting to his sons a bundle of rods. The motto *Insuperabiles si inseparabiles* ("Insuperable if inseparable") would be a commentary on this image. Together, motto and image would symbolize how there was strength in unity. This idea had circulated widely after the events of 1776, and it was one that had already been popular in the emblem books for well over a century.

The emblem above is from an engraving published in 1635 and illustrates how the bear is frustrated in his furious attempts to break one slender shaft, because all the shafts hold together. As the text below the emblem points out, were the shafts divided, the bear "would soone breake them all." Perhaps the choice of thirteen arrows was a reflection of this idea of "strength in unity." There is no surviving evidence to connect the emblem image of 1635 with the arrows in the Great Seal. However, we may be reasonably certain that the importance of the idea rests in the *bundle* of arrows, rather than in any warlike symbolism. In the blazon produced by Charles Thomson in 1782, the arrows are described merely as "a bundle of thirteen arrows," held in the left talon of the eagle.

SOME DEEPER MYSTERIES BEHIND
the
DOLLAR BILL

97. The greatest secret of the dollar bill is in the pyramid roundel.

We have seen that the most reasonable interpretation of the truncated pyramid is related to the idea that the building of America is *a thing still in progress*. It is therefore reasonable to inquire into the symbolism of the irradiated triangle, which seems to "complete" the pyramid.

There is some justification for linking the building of the pyramid with the Christian Scriptures. In the New Testament, we learn how Christ spoke of himself as a *stone*. He was the stone that the builders rejected, yet became "the head of the corner."

In most cases, the several references to this stone have been interpreted as being to a cornerstone, the prime key to the foundation of any building. However, a number of modern scholars have shown that such an interpretation may be inadequate. In certain medieval images, the builders are shown placing the stone on top of the walls, which are thus completed by this addition. This stone was no cornerstone, but a capstone.

Early Christian writings indicate that the stone—which is Christ—was seen as *completing*, as well as founding, the structure of the Church of God. Support for this idea is found in the New Testament. For example, in Matthew 21,

42, the reference in Latin is to the *caput anguli*, which must be translated as "the head of the angle." The word refers to a stone that is being applied to the upper part of the structure. Commenting on this idea, in the fifth century A.D., Saint Augustine of Hippo reminded his readers that cornerstones are found not only in the foundations of buildings but also in their highest parts.

98. The magic of the top of the Egyptian pyramid.

The level of biblical interpretation that we have just examined encourages us to review the intentions behind the image of the unfinished pyramid. Although represented in strictly pagan imagery (the Great Pyramid is among the most ancient of all surviving pagan structures), it was adopted for Christian purposes. This helps explain why a pope should have used the unfinished pyramid as a devise (see 68) and why the pyramid should have become such an important Masonic symbol.

The Egyptians regarded the top of their pyramids with particular veneration. They called the magical capstone, *ben-ben*. The black triangle at the top of the drawing of the pyramid, in the figure at the top of page 51 is nothing other than such a *ben-ben* stone.

One *ben-ben*, or pyramid capstone, has survived from ancient times (see next page). This is the *ben-ben* once used to top the pyramid of Amenemhat III in Dahshur, Egypt. This rare object is now in the Egyptian Museum, Cairo. The drawing shows only the winged *uraeus* (serpent) and eyes—however, the *ben-ben* itself has a large number of hieroglyphics below the wings.

The Egyptian hieroglyphic used to represent the pyramid shows the base, or foundation rock, upon which it is built:

In contrast, as a hieroglyphic, the pure, "unsupported" triangle is visualized as hovering in the air, without foundation:

In the Egyptian hieroglyphics, the triangle marks the beginning of the sacred name for the star Sothis, which was also called Sept:

Sothis is the star that the Greeks named Seirios, meaning "sparkling," or "radiant."

It is the same magnificent binary star that we now call Sirius, in the constellation Canis Major. There is no doubt that this star was the origin of the five-pointed "blazing star" of Masonic symbolism. It is a star that seems to flicker as though it were a burning fire. As the English poet Tennyson wrote:

> And as the fiery Sirius alters hue,
> And bickers into red and emerald, shone
> Their morions, wash'd with morning . . .

If this radiant Sothis star was represented by a triangle, are we not entitled to ask if it is that radiant triangle which completes the truncated pyramid on the dollar bill?

Is it possible that the intense radiations behind the triangle above the incomplete pyramid represent this sparkling Sirius rather than—as is most usually believed—the Sun?

99. The magic numerology of Totten's Seal design.

In some ways, Totten's idealized drawing of the reverse of the Seal on page 49 is slightly absurd. However, from other points of view, it is filled with a deep meaning that is altogether missing in all the Seal designs.

Totten's awareness of the mystique of the radiant star behind the triangle carries the symbolism of the design deep into sacred numerology. Not only does the radiation dominate the roundel, but it even overshines the pyramid itself, thus symbolizing the superiority of the celestial over the earthly forces.

Even more remarkable, this blazing star radiates the space around with thirty-three rays. As we have seen, this is

the number associated with Christ, who lived on earth that number of years (see page 56).

100. The stellar glory on Totten's design.

At first glance, the stellar glory above the eagle on the dollar bill roundel is less dramatic than that we have seen in Totten's design. It has been restrained by the clouds and seems to be nothing more than a backdrop to the thirteen stars.

However, this design was not always so restrained. For proof of this, we must return again to Totten, who represented the obverse and reverse of the Diplomatic Medal on page 150, which had been made following the advice of Thomas Jefferson in 1782.

The reverse shows Mercury offering goods and peace to the representative of America: the medal is dated July 4, 1776. Yet it is neither the reverse symbolism nor the date that interests us here. Our interest lies in the massive sheet of light that irradiates the obverse.

Not only are the stars on this obverse arranged in the same constellational form as on the Great Seal, but, unlike those on the first Great Seal, they are actually five-pointed. This radiant is all-powerful, for it has broken through the clouds and radiates even below the wings of the eagle. Perhaps this "translation" of the Great Seal, coming from the mind of one of the Founding Fathers, is meant to tell us something. Perhaps the design was intended to draw the obvious parallel between the radiant over the pyramid and the radiant over the eagle—pointing the obvious moral that the secret of the two designs is found in Light.

The massive sheet of light in the Diplomatic Medal design is like a triangle reaching down to the triangular form of the eagle, as though seeking to lift it up into the heavens. It is right and proper that the clouds should have no power

to diminish this light, for in truth it is a celestial or spiritual light, which recognizes no material impediment. Just so, the thirteen original stars, arranged within the magical Seal of Solomon, issue a light that the world itself may not diminish or dim.

This radiance may seem to be excessive in terms of that contained within the ring of clouds in the dollar-bill roundel. However, there may be no doubt that in the first proposal for the Seal, drawn up by Du Simitière in 1776, the radiance, or glory, was to spread over almost the whole of the Seal.

The radiant in Totten's imaginative design—like that on the dollar bill—throws its light from a triangle, which was, in the ancient world, a symbol of the crowning of the pyramid. In the modern world, this same triangle is symbol of the

Trinity. Within the triangle is an eye, that was, in the ancient world, the eye of the god *Horus*. In the modern world, this is now the eye of Providence—of the Three-in-One God that looks down providentially on the building of the pyramid below.

This amazing radiant symbolizes the brightest star in the heavens, the most important star in the ancient world. It irradiates the world as a promise of what America may become—a stellar light on earth, and the most important star of the future world.

NOTES

Introduction

The opening quotation is from Charles A. L. Totten, *The Seal of History: Our Inheritance in the Great Seal of "Manasseh," the United States of America. Its History and Heraldry; and Its Signification Unto "The Great People" Thus Sealed* (1897).

Francis Bacon's unfinished fable, *New Atlantis*, was published posthumously in 1626. The imaginary island of Bensalem (which Bacon describes in this work) is a Rosicrucian metaphor for a new politicosocial philosophy.

As we shall see, it is far from easy to separate a study of the symbolism of the dollar bill from that of the Great Seal of the United States. The following works deal specifically with the Seal but, additionally, offer useful insights into the magical background of the dollar bill.

For a work that presents a history of the Great Seal in great detail, and with admiral clarity, see Richard S. Patterson and Richardson Dougall, *The Eagle and the Shield. A History of the Great Seal of the United States* (1976 edn.). This work offers the advantage of an excellent bibliography of works dealing with the Seal and related American symbolism—see pp. 578–606.

For a work that presents the Seal in terms of its magical background, see Robert R. Hieronimus, *An Historical Analysis of the Reverse of the American Great Seal and its Relationship to the Ideology of Humanistic Psychology* (1981), dissertation made available to me in typescript form. See also Robert R. Hieronimus, *America's Secret Destiny: Spiritual Vision & the Founding of a Nation* (1989).

For quirky side issues touching on the Seal, and on American history in general, see also Howard Payson Arnold, *Historic Side Lights* (1899). Other works relating to the Seal and the dollar bill will be mentioned in due course. I have already mentioned the remarkable work by Charles A. L. Totten, *The Seal of History* (1897). This two-volume work contained several errors when it was completed, and time has revealed even more, yet Totten's was a wholesome and energetic search for truth, and his book is still worth a careful read. A number of his insights will be touched upon within the following text.

The Dollar

2. For the conversation between Carol and Bjornstam, see Sinclair Lewis, *Main Street: The Story of Carol Kennicott* (1920, New York, first edn.), p. 115.

3. The quotation relating to *Hungerland*, in which the word *dollar* first appears in English, is from Robert Johnson's translation, *An Historicall description of the most famous kingdomes and Common-weales in the Worlde* (1603). The section on Hungary (*Hungerland*) does not appear in the 1601 edition of this work, and while there are references to many other forms of currency, there is no mention of the dollar.

4. Thomas Jefferson argued for the adoption of the dollar because it was a familiar coinage. See *Works*, vol. III, p. 446. For the dollar as **D**, see *Letter, addressed to the Legislators of the several States composing the Federal Union; Recommending a Uniform Continental Currency.* [Printed in Twenty-first Year of American Independence]. For an example of both the £ and the **D**, in this work, see p. 17.

For the $ symbol, see *Tariff of Duties, on Importations into the Unites States: and Revenue Laws and Custom-House Regulations* (3rd ed., 1824), based on that revised by the Secretary of the Treasury. See, for example, p. 6. Jefferson's use of the pound and dollar symbolism may be seen in several of his papers: for example, in the "Final State of the Report on Weights and Measures," dated July 4, 1790, he uses the £ symbol for pounds, the s symbol for shillings, but either the abbreviations **Doll.** or **D**, for dollar. See *The Papers of Thomas Jefferson*, vol. 16 (edited Julian P. Boyd, 1961), pp. 670–671.

5. The alchemical symbol for Mercury, ☿, which is related to "philosophical" Mercury, appears in the British Library manuscript Harley 2766, entitled *Matheseos sive Astronomicum Librum*. For a general overview of these symbols, see F. Gettings, *Dictionary of Occult, Hermetic and Alchemical Sigils* (1981), pp. 170–71. The serpent-tau symbolism appears in the emblem-book literature: for example, George Wither, *A Collection of Emblems* (1635), book. 1, Emblem xlvii, which points a Christian moral.

6. For the magical numerology of 358 in the context of *nachash* and *Messiah*, see, for example, Charles Poncé, *Kabbalah: An Introduction and Illumination for the World Today* (1974 edn.), pp. 170–71. For the magic of the number 7, see Clio Hogenraad, *Names & Numbers. Their Power and Significance*, (1915), pp.92–96; the quotation is from p. 92.

7. The astrological $ symbol appears, for example, in the British Library manuscript version of Firmicus Maternus, *Matheseos sive Astronomicon Librorum*, pressmark Harley 2766, dated 1510. The astrological-alchemical sigil ℥ is found in the British Library manuscript *Thesaurus Mundi*, dated 1474, pressmark, Add. 15,549. The symbolism in alchemical engravings is, of necessity, well hidden: see however, Sabine Stuart Chevalier, *Discours Philosophique* (1781). I quote this source because, by the time of its publication, the symbolism of the $ was widespread. The relevant plate is conveniently reproduced in Johananes Fabricius, *Alchemy: The Medieval Alchemists and Their Royal Art* (1976), p. 156. An earlier example may be seen in the figure to the right of Mercury, from the second key of Basil Valentine, *Twelve Keys, the Practica cum Duodecim Clavibus* of Michael Maier's *Tripus Aureus*. For an available modern edition of the *Practica*, see Eugène Canseliet, *Les Douze Clefs de la Philosophie* (1956 edn.), p. 111. The mystery of the caduceus is hinted at in plate 7 of Johann Daniel Mylius, *Philosophia Reformata* (1622). In this plate, not only are there two different versions of the caduceus, but the eagle is displayed over the top of the standard form—an extraordinary representation of the relationship held by the Jupiterian bird and the Mercurial sigil. For the entire sequence of engravings, in available form, see Stanislas Klossowski de Rola, *The Golden Game: Alchemical Engravings of the Seventeenth Century*, (1988), pp. 168–177.

The doors of the Bank of England, in London, were designed by Herbert Baker: see his autobiography, *Architecture & Personalities* (1944), which contains a short account of the symbolism of the caduceus and a photograph of the doors.

For the sculpture by John Gregory on the Federal Reserve Board Building in Washington, D.C., see James M. Goode, *The Outdoor Sculpture of Washington*, D.C. (1974), p. 442.

The Dollar Bill and the Seal

8. For an account of Edward M. Weeks's design of the dollar bill, see Patterson and Dougall, *The Eagle and the Shield* (1976 edn.), pp. xxxviii and 407. Quoting a letter from Edward R. Felver, Chief of the Office of Engraving, to Frederick Aandahl, Office of the Historian, in the Department of State, dated February 24, 1977, the authors record that the engraving, on the bill, of the reverse of the Great Seal was undertaken by Joachim Benzing; the obverse of the Seal was engraved by R. Ponickau; and the lettering was engraved by Donald R. McLeod, Edward M. Hall, and William B. Wells.

9. The official reluctance to cut the die for the reverse of the dollar bill does appear to be something of a scandal, even though this reluctance may not be a long-lasting conspiracy, as some individuals suggest. Although Congress did order the cutting of both an obverse and reverse of the Seal, it was evidently their intention, at that time, to use only the obverse. Each of the standard works to which I shall refer here deals with the issue from a variety of standpoints.

The book was Gaillard Hunt, *The History of the Seal of the United States* (1909). This readable work was superseded by Patterson and Dougall, *The Eagle and the Shield* (1976 edn.).

The top of the shield in the dollar-bill roundel has a wide edging. This is not on the Seal of 1904.

The design of the reverse, on page 14, is based on the official design prepared for the Department of State in 1972. It therefore had the pyramid on the dollar bill as one of its graphic guides. There are a large number of differences between the two. Most notably, the 1972 design has a different number of blocks in the makeup of the pyramid: there are seventy-nine distinct blocks in the 1972 design. The bottom corners of the pyramids are aligned to different letters in the motto. The ends of banderols of the 1972 design extend higher in relation to the pyramid than those in the dollar roundel. The bifurcated ends of the banderols on the 1972 design are quite different from those in the dollar bill. The eye of the 1972 design is clearly a left eye; that in the dollar roundel has been represented in such a way that one cannot determine with any certainty to which side of the face it belongs.

10. Franklin D. Roosevelt became a Master Mason in November 1911, in Holland Lodge No. 8, New York—the same lodge of which George Washington had been an honorary member, when inaugurated first President in 1789. In 1935— the year Roosevelt authorized the printing of the new dollar bill—his sons Franklin D. Jr. and James became Masons in Architect Lodge No. 517, New York, in the presence of their father.

Henry Morgenthau Jr. was made a Mason in April 1922 in the Obed Lodge No. 984, Poughkeepsie, New York.

Henry A. Wallace was made a Mason in October 1927 in Capital Lodge No. 110, Des Moines, Iowa.

11. The letters of Henry A. Wallace and his correspondents that refer to Wallace's interest in the design of the Seal and to his subsequent role in suggesting the idea to Roosevelt are in the Wallace Papers, at the University of Iowa. I consulted the copies in the Manuscript Division of the Library of Congress (microfilm reel 46).

12. William Barton was born in Philadephia in 1754, and was of Anglo-Irish descent. His mother was one of the sisters of David Rittenhouse, the first director of the United States Mint, in Philadelphia. Barton studied law in England and was admitted to the bar of the Pennsylvania Supreme Court in 1779. In 1782, he was invited to design the Great Seal, for the approval of

Congress—perhaps this invitation was initiated because of his known interest in heraldry. He authored a number of books: of interest, even today, is his biography of Rittenhouse, *Memoirs of the Life of David Rittenhouse, LLD., F.R.S.* (1813). Barton died in the borough of Lancaster in 1817.

For a good work on Thomson's life, see Lewis R. Harley, *The Life of Charles Thomson, Secretary of the Continental Congress and Translator of the Bible from the Greek* (1900).

Pierre Eugène Du Simitière was born in Geneva, Switzerland, in 1737. He had sailed to America in about 1763 and spent some years in New York, during which time he traveled widely, visiting other colonist cities. During this time, he earned a living doing portraits and portrait silhouettes, maps, and general jobbing design. In 1769, he became a naturalized citizen of New York, but five years later, settled in Philadelphia. He was an avid collector—the first to establish a collection of American history pertaining to the colonies: his American Museum was being advertised as early as 1782. He was on friendly terms with Franklin, Jefferson, and Adams; this may have been one reason why he was invited to serve as artist for the First Committee, convened in 1776 to consider the design of the Great Seal. Another reason was that he had already had some experience designing medals.

13–14. Details of the contribution made by Robert Scot to engraving in the United States appear in Patterson and Dougall, *The Eagle and the Shield* (1976 edn.) (see esp. pp. 112–22). Scot is listed in the Philadelphia city directories between 1785 and 1822, and was working in that city as an engraver by 1821. From contemporaneous comments, it is evident that Scot was highly regarded as an engraver. Evidence for Scot's connection with the Great Seal hinges on a reference to him in a postscript to a letter written by Charles

Thomson to his wife (then in Philadelphia) on April 3, 1785. In this, Thomson asks her to ensure that Scot received an account for engraving the seal (which we assume is the Great Seal). The letter is preserved among the Charles Thomson Papers in the Manuscript Division of the Library of Congress. According to Patterson and Dougall, op. cit., p. 114, the importance of this postscript in reference to the Seal was first noted by Dr. Lee H. Burke of the Office of the Historian, Department of State.

Robert Scot was probably born in Edinburgh (Scotland) in 1745, and was certainly living in the United States by 1778. In 1781, Thomas Jefferson (then governor of Virginia) commissioned him to engrave a number of medals for presentation to Indian chieftains. At about this time, Scot moved to Philadelphia: it is possible that he cut the Great Seal die in his workshop on Front Street, next door to the corner of Vine Street. In 1793, Scot was appointed by George Washington (probably on the recommendation of David Rittenhouse, the director of the Mint) as engraver to the Mint of the United States. He died in Philadelphia in 1823. Scot was a Mason and Quaker.

15. The Seal die of 1782 is on display in the main exhibition hall of the National Archives in Washington, D.C.

The engraving of the Seal design (replete with five-pointed stars) was made by James Trenchard for the *Columbian Magazine*, entitled, "Description of the Arms of the United States" (September 1786), pp. 33–34.

For Thomson's *Remarks and Explanation* of the Seal proposal (which are among the Papers of the Continental Congress, item 49), see Patterson and Dougall, *The Eagle and the Shield* (1976 edn.), p. 84–85.

The term *Jonathan arrows* is derived from the Bible: they are so called after the hero Jonathan, mentioned in I Samuel 20:35–38.

16. John P. V. N. Throop worked in Boston c.1828 and in Washington, D.C., from about 1830. He died in Washington, D.C., in 1860, and is buried in the Congressional Cemetery there. He was an engraver, lithographer, portrait painter, and painter of miniatures.

Although Throop was probably working to official instructions while cutting this die, it was he who introduced the five-pointed star to the Seal. He deviated from the congressional orders by representing only six arrows instead of the specified thirteen: as Hunt, *The History of the Seal of the United States* (1909), p. 48, has pointed out, this omission made the Seal "illegal." Throop delivered the newly cut die to the custodianship of the Secretary, Daniel Webster, in 1841. It was in use until 1877.

17. Herman Baumgarten's die, cut and first used in 1877, continued the Throop error of the six arrows, but introduced thirteen cloud clusters around the constellations. It has been recognized by a number of historians that the commissioning and use of this die were done with little public notice. As Patterson and Dougall (op. cit., p. 226) point out, this may have been due to the wish of the Department of State to avoid attracting attention to the deficiencies in the Baumgarten Seal and its immediate predecessor. Some of the deficiencies had been discussed by John D. Champlin in his article "The Great Seal of the United States: Concerning Some Irregularities in It," *The Galaxy* (May 1877). The whereabouts of the Baumgarten die is unknown.

Herman Baumgarten was an engraver of Seals, stamps, and stencils. He had been born in Hanover in 1849 and emigrated to the United States with his family at the age of three, settling in Baltimore. After learning and practicing his trade (which was also that of his father), he moved to Washington, D.C. in 1871, where he became the most proficient and prolific of governmental seal engravers.

18. The die for the Tiffany design was long presumed lost. However, in 1976, it was discovered in a cupboard in the Presidential Commissions Office. Sometime prior to December 1883, the well-known firm of jewelers, Tiffany & Company, was approached by Theodore F. Dwight, chief of the Bureau of Rolls and Library of the State Department, and in that same month, Tiffany provided two designs for the reverse. These sketchy drawings are preserved in the National Archives in Washington, D.C. (Record Group 59, entry 855). They restore the thirteen arrows and altogether miss the numerology of the stones on the pyramid. The work of redesigning the Seal die was given to Tiffany & Company, and this work appears to have been overseen by James Horton Whitehouse.

Whitehouse was born in Handsworth, England, in 1833, and emigrated to the United States in 1857. He was employed by Tiffany & Company in the following year. He died in Brooklyn in 1902.

Prior to designing the die, advice was invited from a number of specialist historians, who made it their duty to examine the extant documentation relating to the Seal. It is arguable as to the extent to which this advice was heeded. This Tiffany die was used as the fiducial for the later Seal of 1904, which now figures on the dollar bill. It was the first design to make use of thirteen olives on the olive branch (a personal triumph for Charles A. L. Totten, who had campaigned vigorously for this symbolism, to meet the specification set out by Congress in 1782). The cloud formation around the constellation appears to consist of twenty separate nebulae.

19. The Zeitler die of 1904 replaced the Tiffany die, which had become worn after only nineteen years' use. The die was

ordered from Bailey Banks & Biddle of Philadelphia, and was cut in that city by the engraver Max Zeitler. The general effect of this beautiful design may be seen on the eagle roundel of the dollar bill. The precision with which Zeitler cut the radiants between the clouds and the constellation (his purpose being to represent exactly the heraldic colors) has been lost in the bill engraving, mainly because of the small space available. However, a careful count of Zeitler's design, based on a surviving impression, reveals twenty-five lines and sixty-five dots. The lines were intended to represent the heraldic azure (the blue of the sky), while the dots were intended to represent heraldic gold. Zeitler made the cloud formations into nineteen recognizable nebulae. The authors Patterson and Dougall, op. cit., have suggested that the print of the obverse of the Seal, made famous by Gaillard Hunt in his work *The History of the Seal of the United States* (1909), reproduced here on page 14, may have been a direct copy of the drawing Zeitler made during his preparation of his die for the Seal.

Max Zeitler was born in Frankfurt am Main in 1854, and studied engraving in Germany. In 1888, he emigrated to the United States, where he immediately found work with Bailey, Banks & Biddle, in Philadelphia. An amusing footnote to history is that when Zeitler had completed his work on the die, dominated by the American eagle, he renamed his own private engraving firm Eagle Engraving Company. He died in Philadelphia in 1922.

The Stars of the Dollar Bill

20–21. The Confederatio coin is from Totten, op. cit., p. 247. The notion that the inverted five-pointed star was *evil* seems to have been popularized by the nineteenth-century

French occult journalist Eliphas Lévi, who knew less about magic symbols than he pretended. See, for example, Lévi, *Dogme et Rituel de la Haute Magie*, in the English version of A. E. Waite, *Transcendental Magic* (1896), p. 227. An example of the adoption of the grotesque Lévi teaching concerning the inverted star, in what is otherwise a sensible appraisal of the star, may be seen in William B. Greene, *The Blazing Star; with an Appendix Treating of the Jewish Kabbala* (1872), p. 9.

As a matter of fact, the inverted five-pointed star proliferates in American art. There is an example on the shield in the painting of arms and armor by James Leslie (to the design of Constantino Brumidi) on the wall of the Senate Appropriations Committee Room, S-128. Another example is on the sculpture *Wisdom* by Lee Lawrie, above the doors of the south entry of the Senate Chamber in the Capitol Building, Washington, D.C.

22. The six-pointed star, formed from the interlinked triangles, has many names. These include the Shield of David, the Seal of Solomon, the Insignet of Hermes, the Seal of the Prince of Peace, and the [seal of the] Builder of the Two Paths. The detail of the Jewish amulet (left, on page 28) is from the *Sepher Raziel*, reproduced in full, with a useful analysis, by E. A. Wallis Budge, *Amulets and Superstitions* (1930), p. 226. The variant to the right is from the Theosophical symbol designed by Helena P. Blavatsky in New York in 1875; for this "hieroglyphic," see J. C. Street, *The Hidden Way Across the Threshold, or The Mystery which hath been Hidden for Ages and from Generations* (1887), p. 47. Towards the end of the nineteenth century, the swastika (in the second diagram) had none of the evil associations later foisted upon it by the Nazis: in this context, it was derived from Buddhist symbolism.

23. In the upper left of the central star of the seal of Oklahoma is a seven-pointed star. There are several works that

reproduce the seals of the states: easily available is the American History Research Associates publication, Vincent Wilson, *The Book of the States* (1986 edn.). See also George Earlie Shankle, *State Names, Flags, Seals, Rings, Birds, Flowers and Other Symbols* (1938 edn.), pp. 181–256.

24. The arms of Sulgrave Manor and the Washington bookplate are reproduced from Totten, *The Seal of History*, vol. 1, p. 33. The finest collection of the Washington family arms is preserved in the stained glass of the church of St. Mary the Virgin at Fawsley (opposite Fawsley Hall), a few miles from Sulgrave.

The early seal of Maryland has an interesting history. Only the reverse is used for official business. The obverse is used only for decorative purposes: this latter depicts Lord Baltimore as a knight on a charger. The reverse (reproduced here) replaced that used until 1776, based on the arms of the Calverts and Crosslands. In 1876, the earlier arms were adopted once more, and are still in use, bearing the earliest date (1632) on any state seal. For an account of the Maryland seal, see George Earlie Shankle, *State Names, Flags, Seals, Rings, Birds, Flowers and Other Symbols* (1938 edn.), pp. 196–97.

25. Thomson's sketch is preserved in the National Archives, in *Papers of the Continental Congress*, Item 23, folio 180, Record Group 360, The engravings of the Constellatio coins are from Sylvester S. Crosby, *The Early Coins of America; and the Laws Governing Their Issue* (1875), pp. 331ff.

26. For the Egyptian *sba* star, see E. A. Wallis Budge, *An Egyptian Hieroglyphic Dictionary* (1920), p. cxxv. The reproduction of the *sba* in the name of goddess, Isis Sept, above the figure in this section is from Sir J. Gardner Wilkinson, *The Manners and Customs of the Ancient Egyptians* (1878), vol. I, plate 26.

Among the most striking *sba*-star ceilings is that in the supposed burial chamber in the pyramid of Unas. An excellent color photograph is in Werner Forman and Stephen Quirke, *Hieroglyphics and the Afterlife in Ancient Egypt* (1996), p. 55.

27. An account of the circumstances surrounding the production of the Hog money of the Sommer Islands (the coins were not "minted," but "struck") is in *Early American Coins. Ch. 1. British Coinage in America: Autonomous Issues, i. Sommer Islands [Bermuda] [1615–1616]*," pp. 9–10. See also Crosby, *The Early Coins of America and the Laws Governing Their Issue* (1875), pp. 1–18. There is a small collection of Hog coins in the Numismatic Department of the Smithsonian Institution, Washington, D.C.

28. I have borrowed the detail of Bacon's arms from the portrait frontispiece of Edwin Durning-Lawrence, *Bacon Is Shakespeare* (1910).

William Shakespeare's reference to the Bermudas is in *The Tempest*, act 1, scene ii, 1.229. When he wrote this play, the islands were named after the Spanish sea captain Juan de Bermudez. Although the Elizabethan and Jacobean audiences would have been delighted by the connection Shakespeare drew between the "real-life" shipwreck and his own drama, this connection seems to have been forgotten in the following century. It was rediscovered by the Shakespearean scholar Edmond Malone; see *An Account of the Incident, from which the Title and Part of the Story of Shakespeare's Tempest were derived, and its True Date Ascertained* (1808).

In 1609, they were renamed the Somers Islands in honor of the British Admiral Sir George Somers, whose ship, carrying settlers to Virginia, put in there after sustaining hurricane damage. The wild hogs, brought originally by the Spanish, had flourished there— hence, one reason for the name of the island and the coinage.

The reports sent to the Virginia Company in England were so enthusiastic about the Somers Islands that the Company had their charter amended to incorporate them. Thus becoming part of the colony, they were promptly renamed Virginiola and were colonized by the Virginia Company in 1612. Later, the group was called the Summer Island.

29. The detail of the shaman engraving is from a print of 1591 by Theodore de Bry, after a drawing made by the French artist Jacques le Moyne de Morgues. Le Moyne had been a member of the disastrous expedition to Florida, undertaken on the orders of Charles IX in 1564. The plate illustrates how Chief Outina, witnessed by the French, consults a sorcerer in order to determine in advance how many of the enemy they would encounter and the place where they would fight. For a full account of the production of the Florida drawings and engravings, see Stefan Lorant, *The New World: The First Pictures of America Made by John White and Jacques le Moyne and Engraved by Theodore de Bry* (1946).

30. There is a considerable number of books dealing with the history and symbolism of the national flag. A standard work is George Henry Preble, *Origin and History of the American Flag* (1917 edn.), 2 vols: the flag reproduced in this section is from p. 282 of this work: it represents the flag of the *Bon Homme Richard*, said to have been displayed during her action with the *Serapis* in September 1779. A shorter work is Charles W. Stewart, *The Stars and Stripes from Washington to Wilson 1777–1914* (1914). For some examples of beautiful early flags, see B. & M-L d'Otrange Mastai, *The Stars and Stripes: The American Flag as Art and as History from the Birth of the Republic to the Present* (1973).

31. The ring has been adapted from Catarus, *Le Imagine degli Dei degli Antichi* (1608), p. 91, where it is called the *Segno della Salute* (symbol of health).

The numerological link between the number 5 and rebirth is very well established in traditional magic: in popular lore, it may be confirmed from Clio Hogenraad, *Names and Numbers. Their Power and Significance*, (1915), p. 86.

For Jesus and the pentagram, see, for example, the so-called *Tycho Brahe Calendar*, edited and published by Adam McLean, *The Magical Calendar* (1979), in the Magnum Opus Hermetic Sourceworks series. In the corresponding amuletic form, represented in the Magical Calendar attributed to the arcanists, Trithemius of Spanheim and his pupil, Agrippa of Nettesheim. Christ is shown crucified against the five-pointed star, and stands resurrected in front of the Seal of Solomon, or six-pointed star. For a good reproduction of these, see the *Calendarium Naturale Magicum* in Appendix V of Karl Anton Nowotny, *Henricus Cornelius Agrippa ab Nettesheym, De Occulta Philosophia* (1967), pp. 615 and 618.

32. The pentagrammic man is from Cornelius Agrippa, *De Occulta Philosophia* (1534), book. II, p. clxiii. The Anglo-Saxon names of the days, based on the pagan gods, were: *Monandæg, Tiwesdæg, Wodensdæg, Thuresdæg, Frigedæg, Saterdæg*, and *Sunnandæg*. For an interesting study of the planetary background to the names of the days, see J. C. H., "On the Names of the Days of the Week," in *The Philological Museum*, vol. 1, no. 1 (1832), pp. 1–73.

33. Jefferson Davis's description of the stars as symbolizing "endless existence and heavenly birth" is in a letter dated January 15, 1856, which he wrote, from the War Department to Meigs. See Thomas Hicks, *Eulogy on Thomas Crawford* (1865), p. 86. The correspondence and original photographs are now in the Library of the Architect of the Capitol, Washington, D.C.

In her *Memoir* of her husband, Mrs. Davis recorded that, besides studying classics and the usual academic subjects of the day, Davis had also been educated in "profane and sacred history." Perhaps it is from the latter literature that he intuited the magical significance of the five-pointed star. See *Jefferson Davis, Ex-President of the Confederate States of America: A Memoir* (1890), I, p. 27.

The statue proved to be Thomas Crawford's last work. He died in London on October 10, 1857. By a strange coincidence, the news of Crawford's death reached the United States simultaneously with the arrival of the ship containing his colossal bronze statue of George Washington, intended for Richmond. His *Freedom* was cast in the foundry of Clark Mills, in Washington, D.C., in the following year. It was not erected until December 2, 1863, when (as Abraham Lincoln hoped) the ceremony would provide inspiration for the dispirited Union troops.

The story of the making of *Freedom* is told in Robert L. Gale, *Thomas Crawford. American Sculptor* (1964).

34. See Schuyler Hamilton, *The History of the National Flag of the United States of America* (1853). One might be tempted to mock Schuyler Hamilton for his attempt to identify the constellation mentioned in the blazon. One of Hamilton's arguments was that in 1820, John Quincy Adams, Secretary of State, had authorized a new design for the American passport. This incorporated a circle of fourteen stars around an eagle, which held in its beak an image of the harplike Lyra. This musical instrument was itself studded with thirteen stars. Adams was familiar with the implications behind his intriguing device, for he wrote at length about it in his *Memoirs* (see IV, pp. 233ff). The motto on this device, *Nunc Sidera Ducit* ("now it leads the stars"), is from the astrological poem of the Roman poet Manilius, *Astronomica,* in the G. P. Gould trans., p. 30, line 329. His symbolism was aimed at representing the star Wega as the equivalent of America, leading the other nations.

The extraordinary fact is that William Barton's artwork, for his second visualization of the Seal, does suggest he had in mind that one of the groups of thirteen stars in this design was a fiducial (or guide star), for this was much larger than the rest. The artwork is too delicate to be reproduced with sufficient accuracy to reveal this fiducial. All the line drawings known to me are inaccurate. However, I have examined this striking artwork in person, and vouch for what I claim above.

If William Barton was so inclined to visualize the constellation as a *particular* stellar figure, with a fiducial, then it behooves us to ask what this prime star might have been. We need not attempt to answer this question here, but the very fact that this question may be asked should lead us to consider Adam's proposition in a new light. Perhaps the prime star was meant to represent Wega, and perhaps the constellation intended was *Aquila Cadens* (the Swooping Eagle). In the Euphratean star lists, the bird known as the eagle was also called the Living Eye. In the incomplete gores from the Johann Schöner star map, which was found with the Waldseemüller world map, the eagle is represented under its old name, *Vultur Cadens*.

As the image from Hamilton's work, on page 43, suggests, the constellation Lyra, of which Wega is the prime star, was frequently represented in the old star maps as being held in the claws of this eagle. For these stars and constellations, see Richard Hinckley Allen, *Star Names: Their Lore and Meaning* (1966 unabridged ed. of the 1899 *Star-Names and Their Meanings*), under "Lyra" (pp. 280ff).

The Eye of Providence

35. Pierre Eugene Du Simitière's sketch is now in the Manuscript Division of the Library of Congress, among the

Thomas Jefferson Papers. I have used the tracing reproduced by Arnold, *Historic Side-Lights* (1899) opp. p. 282.

Benjamin Franklin was made a Mason in February 1731, at St. John's Lodge, Philadelphia. On June 24, 1755, he was among those Masons who dedicated the first Masonic building in America—the Free-Masons' Lodge in Philadelphia.

The Eye within a triangle, enclosed within a blazing Star, which is reproduced in this section, is from an isolated tear sheet from a French Masonic pamphlet, dated 1766, in the author's collection. The Masonic "Royal Arch" plate, with seven five-pointed stars and a blazing star in the shape of a comet, is from John Fellows, *Exposition of the Mysteries, or Religious Dogmas and Customs of the Ancient Egyptians, Pythagoreans and Druids* (1835). The text explains the blazing star as Anubis, the Dog Star, and puts forward the proposition that this star (in fact, our Sirius) "has descended to the Freemasons."

36. Benson J. Lossing's "realization" was published in "The Great Seal of the United States," in *Harper's New Monthly Magazine*, in July 1856 [vol. XIII, June to November, pp. 178–186], along with a number of engravings relating to the history of the Seal—not all of these being accurate representations. Although written in the form of fiction, and aptly described by Arnold, *Historical Side-Lights* (1899) p. 283 as being "copiously bespangled with many specious and pleasing delusions of his vivid imagination," this has influenced many later "histories" of the Seal.

37–38. Barton's design of 1782 was executed in water color and is now preserved in the National Archives. It is not normally on public display.

39. The Egyptian pyramid with *udjats* is from Wilkinson's book, *Manners and Customs of the Ancient Egyptians*, 1841, plate 85 [not marked as such]. For the various forms of the

Asari (Osiris) symbolism (of eye and throne), and for a survey of the symbolism of the all-seeing God, see E. A. Wallis Budge, *Osiris and the Egyptian Resurrection*, (1911), esp. chap. II, "The Name and Iconography of Osiris," pp. 24–61.

40. The woodcut of "Egyptian Hieroglyphics" is from Francesco Colonna, *Hypnerotomachia Poliphili* (1499).

41. The illustration, after an ancient Egyptian papyrus, depicting the baboon of Thoth restoring the eye to the Moon god, is from Wallis Budge, *Amulets and Superstitions* (1930), p. 141.

42–43. The engraved plate in section 43 is from the frontispiece to Jacob Boehme, *Von der Menschwerdung Jesu Christi*, in *Theosophische Wercken* (1623).

The number 33 was widely adopted into the symbolism of Christian art. See, for example, Carlo Crivelli's *Annunciation, with Saint Emidius*, no. 739, in the National Gallery, London; there are thirty-three complete eyes on the tail of the peacock, above the head of Mary (the incomplete eyes behind the bird's wings must be ignored in this count).

Jacob Boehme was born in Alt-Sedenberg in 1575, and became a shoemaker by trade. In 1612, he had an illumination, in consequence of which he began to write his mystical works. His first work was declared heretical, and he was ordered to stop writing in such a way. However, he continued to write, and was soon recognized as one of the remarkable mystics of the early seventeenth century. Boehme was the spiritual connection that links Paracelsian alchemy and esotericism with eighteenth-century mysticism. He appears to have been involved in the Rosicrucian movement, and his approach to arcane matters influenced the early symbolism of the Freemasons. His most profound spiritual influence appears to have been on the English poet William Blake. Boehme died in 1624.

44. For Robert Moray as a Mason and his extensive use of the five-pointed star, see David Stevenson, *The Origins of Freemasonry: Scotland's Century 1590-1710* (2001 edn.) esp. pp. 166ff. The distinctive signature of Moray, reproduced in this section, is copied from a letter written from the royal palace at Whitehall (London) on October 4, [16]72. In this, Moray presents to the Earl of Essex one Mr. Henderson, in the hope that the Earl might be able to find the latter employment. The two parts of Moray's "eye" seal, which have been placed together in this section, are from this letter, which is now in the British Library manuscript collection, pressmark, Stow 200, f. 299-300. For the American Masons Forbes and Skene, see Stevenson, op. cit., pp. 203-204. Few Scottish Masons (operative or otherwise) could fail to be aware of that extraordinary building at Rosslyn, which was richly decorated with five-pointed stars, at that time called mullets.

45. The sculptor of the Charles I medal of 1648 was Nicholas Burghers: see Edward Hawkins, *Medallic Illustrations of the History of Great Britain and Ireland, to the Death of George II* (1885), pp. 333-37.

46. The engravings of the Vermont coins are from Crosby, *The Early Coins of America; and the Laws Governing their Issue* (1875), p. 180. Those of the *Nova Constellatio* are from Crosby, op. cit., p. 331.

47-49. Rembrandt Peale's portrait of George Washington (the so-called *Porthole Portrait*) in the Office of the Vice President in the Capitol in Washington, D.C., is emblazoned with the Latin title, *Patriae Pater*—Father of the Country.

It is sometimes said that Gilbert Stuart made so many copies of what is now called the *Athenaeum Portrait* (commissioned by Martha Washington) that no one has been able to count them. If the engravings are added to this list, then there is probably some truth in the claim. There are two painted copies in the Capitol in Washington, D.C. One, the *Thomas Chestnut Portrait*, is in the main corridor of the Senate wing. Another, the *Edward Pennington Portrait*, is in the Office of Senate Majority Leader. A third (formerly owned by Mr. Phelps of Boston) was destroyed in the fire that gutted the library in 1851. Stuart had learned the art of painting in England, notably, under Benjamin West: he painted the portraits of three European kings (Louis XVI, George III, and George IV, while still Prince of Wales). After his return to the United States in 1792, he executed from life the portraits of six Presidents. These were George Washington, John Adams, Thomas Jefferson, James Madison, James Monroe, and John Quincy Adams. See Charles E. Fairman, *Art and Artists of the Capitol of the United States of America* (1927), pp. 273–75. See also Gustavus A. Eisen, *Portraits of Washington*, 1932.

Specifically in regard to 47, it is worth observing that the portraits on the other bills are not designed to incorporate the omega symbolism. Nor are the eyes of those portrayed at the center of the bill. For example, I have before me the five- and ten-dollar bills, 1999 series. The portrait of Abraham Lincoln, on the five-dollar bill, is so arranged that his right eye falls on one of the diagonals of the design, but it is nowhere near the center. Likewise, on the ten-dollar bill, neither of the eyes of Hamilton is anywhere near the center of the design.

The Word "America"

50. Among the more questionable arcane references to the word *America* is the claim made by H. P. Blavatsky that the name was derived from the pre-Nicaraguan *Americ*. This, and almost everything Blavatsky claimed about the etymology of

America, is inaccurate. She claimed, for example, that Amerigo Vespucci was called Albericus. As a matter of fact, the 1507 Latin of the Waldseemüller map gives his Latinized name as Americus Vesputium: but, of course, the map was not discovered until after the death of Blavatsky. For Blavatsky's various confusions, see, for example, *Isis Unveiled,* (1877), vol. I, p. 591ff. I mention this source mainly because many of her claims have been drawn into the Theosophical literature and have spilled over into popular occultism. Beneath the portrait by Constantino Brumidi, on the ceiling of the President's Room in the Senate Wing of the Capitol Building, Washington, D.C., are the words AMERICUS VESPUCIUS. Blavatsky would have had an opportunity to see this painting.

A single surviving edition of the Waldseemüller map was discovered in 1901 by Josef Fischer in the library of Wolfegg Castle. For details, see "The Waldseemüller World Map: A Typographic Appraisal," in *Imago Mundi,* no. 37 (1985), pp. 30–51.

The magical use of the letter A does not always distinguish the Hebraic, Christian, and Greek traditions. However, there may be no doubt that the magical import of A has been intensified by the Jewish literature, relating to the first *Sephirah,* which is the Crown. This symbolism is linked with the light aleph (*aleph lucidum*) and the dark aleph (*aleph tenebrosum*), which is, in turn, associated with the beginning and end of the letter A, as seen in such a word as AMERICA. For the primal symbolism, see Thomas Vaughan, *Anthroposophia Theomagia* (1650). Curiously enough (and this may not have been intentional on the part of the designers), the letter A in the word DOLLAR at the bottom of the reverse of the bill *does* combines the light form of the letter and the shadow form, such as was favored in certain Rosicrucian vignettes of the Elizabethan and Jacobean periods. This symbolism is expressed hermetically in the crossed compass and square of the Masons, in which the compass is "light," the square "dark." The crossing of these two working tools produces at the center a lozenge, symbol of the sacred Quintessence, rather than the triangle (Trinity) that figures in the unadorned letter A.

51. The biblical references to the words attributed to the Lord God, *I am the Alpha and Omega,* figured widely in medieval art. However, many modern biblical scholars point out that there is no certain evidence that these were the words of God himself. Personally, I cannot see that such words would have any significance whatsoever, without they were issued by either God or Christ. The references are found in Revelation 1:8, 21:6, and 22:13. The equivalent text, referent to alpha and omega in the King James version of Revelation 1:11, seems to be a later textual insert, for it is not found in the earliest Greek versions of Revelation. Comparison of these sources, with the lapidary script from Saint-Bénigne, in the Dijon Museum, recorded on page 69, indicates that the Latin text is not, in the strictest terms, from the Bible itself, but is a pastiche.

The portrait of Christ was copied from the Commodilla catacombs (entrance via delle Sette Chiese, Rome), which is usually dated to the fourth century A.D.

52–54. The use of the angles projected by words beginning and ending in the upper case A may be seen, in modern times, in the logo for AREA, the Autoroute Rhône-Alpes, reproduced in Adrian Frutiger, *Type Sign Symbol* (n.d.), p. 106. The plate from Jacob Boehme is the frontispiece to his *Von der Gnaden Wahl,* from the *Theosophische Wercken* (1682).

55. The magical significance of the number 13 is best examined in the popular "numerological" texts, where the associations are usually stripped bare of the intellectual justifications

that lay behind them. From Clio Hogenraad, *Names and Numbers: Their Power and Significance*, (1915), pp. 115–17, we may derive the following adages:

> 13 . . . is a capstone number.
> 13 . . . feels the truth of spiritual things, possessing inner knowledge of them . . .
> 13 . . . is full of life and integrity.
> 13 is called a prosperous and not an unlucky number, which is a tradition from the ancient people. . . . [It] is a number of evolution and progress . . . a sacred number and a messenger from another world.

The Mottoes

56–57. The phrase *ex pluribus unum* is from Augustine, *Confessions*, book IV, chap. 8. For some interesting insights on the version *E pluribus unum*, see Arnold, op. cit., pp. 289–292. With some humor (and with some justification), Arnold traces the motto of Pierre-Antoine Motteux to the cruel intolerance and bigotry of Louis XIV of France, who revoked the Edict of Nantes. A little-known philosophical and theological text that alerted American intellectuals to the power of this idea of "the many in the one" was *The Philosophical and Mathematical Commentaries of Proclus, on the First Book of Euclid's Elements* (1792), vol. I, pp. 321ff.

58. The motto reproduced on page 83 is from *The Gentleman's Journal* for January 1692. Pierre-Antoine Motteux was a fine scholar. He produced a translation of the works of the French author Rabelais that is still highly regarded. For an appreciation, see W. F. Smith, *Rabelais: The Five Books and*

Minor Writings (1893), pp. xv–xix. Motteux was murdered in London in 1718. The poet Dryden, who had been his friend, wrote a valedictory poem, ending:

> Words, once my stock, are wanting to commend
> So great a poet and so good a friend.

59. The New Jersey copper coin of 1786 is from Totten, op. cit.

60. The motto *Annuit Coeptis* is from Virgil's *Aeneid* [book 9, line 625]: *Juppiter omnipotens, audacibus annue coeptis* ("Omnipotent Jupiter, favor our daring enterprise"). A similar line is also found in Virgil's Georgics, book I, line 40: *Da facilem cursum, atque audacibus annue coeptis* ("Give a smooth path, look kindly on my daring enterprise"). The Seal motto is a loose adaptation of the original Virgil, and means "He favors our undertaking"—the implication being that the undertaking is daring.

61. The Latin motto *Novus Ordo Seclorum* ("A new order of the Ages") is from Virgil's *Eclogue* IV, line 5. This *Eclogue* was interpreted by many as being a prophecy of the coming of Christ: the modern translator of the *Eclogues*, Guy Lee, refers to it as "the famous Messianic *Eclogue*" (see Guy Lee, *Virgil: The Eclogues* [1984 edn.], p. 55). The original words read, *magnus ab integro saeclorum nascitur ordo* ("the great series of ages is born anew"). It has been shown that this line does not refer to the Great Year, relating to the planetary periods, but to "a world endlessly redeemed." See Wendell Clausen, *A Commentary on Virgil Eclogues* (1994), p. 131. The words, as adopted on the Seal, appear to have enthused Shelley, for he used them in his last chorus from *Hellas* (1822):

> The world's great age begins anew,
> The golden years return . . .

62. I record this spelling of *seclorum* as being of dubious orthography. In fact, it did appear in this form, in certain editions of Virgil probably known to Thomson. However, Thomson and his associates were far too learned as classical scholars not to know that the more usual spelling was *saeclorum*: furthermore, they were far too intent on a suitable republican symbolism not to see the numerical value of *seclorum*, as against that of *saeclorum*. For a survey, see Patterson and Dougall, *The Eagle and the Shield* (1976 edn.), pp. 90–91. It is worth recording that, of the three texts of the *Eclogue* from my own shelves or notebooks, and of the three scholarly works on Virgil from the same sources, the word *saeclorum* is used exclusively. These works are: Wendell Clausen, *A Commentary on Virgil Eclogues*, (1994), p. 131; R. A. B. Mynors, *P. Vergili Maronis Opera* (1969), p. 10 ; Thomas F. Royds, *The Eclogues, Bucolics, or Pastorals of Virgil*, (1922), p. 42; Philip Hardie (ed.), *Virgil: Critical Assessments of Classical Authors* (1999), p. 257. R. S. Conway et al., *Virgil's* Messianic Eclogue (1907), *Ecloga IV*, 1.5; Richard F. Thomas, *Reading Virgil and His Texts: Studies in Intertextuality* (1999), p. 103.

63. Totten, *The Seal of History* (1897), must have misread the number of courses on the pyramid from the tabulations provided by Piazzi Smyth in *Our Inheritance in the Great Pyramid* (1880 edn., which Totten probably used): the number of courses on the complete structure is given as 211, including the capstone (see Smyth, op. cit., pp. 94–95). The illustration of the pyramid roundel on this page is from Totten, op.cit., vol. 2, p. 265.

Charles Piazzi Smyth, born in Naples, Italy, in 1819, was made Astronomer Royal for Scotland in 1845. His survey of the Great Pyramid, undertaken in 1638 and 1639, led to several books on the subject, all of which were interspersed with mystical speculations as to the biblical significance of the structures. Smyth confirmed that the entrance passage of the Great Pyramid was oriented to the star Alpha Draconis in the third millennium B.C. Smyth died in 1900: his grave, in St. John's churchyard, Sharow (North Yorkshire), is in the form of the Great Pyramid. The influence of Smyth on Masonry was considerable: see, for example, Rowland Allan Brangwin, *"The Bible in Stone,"* or, *The Great Pyramid the Foundation of Freemasonry"* (1881).

64. The motto *In God We Trust* was suggested by the Secretary of the Treasury, Salmon P. Chase, in December 1863, in consequence of the benign agitation, begun two years earlier, of the Reverend M. R. Watkinson of Ridleyville, Pennsylvania. Watkinson had perceived the need for a national motto that recognized the importance of God in the affairs of the United States. The motto (chosen from several possible appropriate mottoes) was first adopted on a two-cent coin, consequent to an act of Congress passed on April 22, 1864. A bill that was passed by the Senate and approved by the President on July 11, 1955, made the motto mandatory on all currency of the United States. A further resolution, passed in the House on April 16 and in the Senate on July 23, received the President's approval on July 30, 1956, that the motto *In God We Trust* should be the national motto of the United States. An excellent survey of the development of the motto is given by Patterson and Dougall, *The Eagle and the Shield* (1976 edn.) pp. 514–520.

The replacement of the three five-pointed stars by the English motto in the House Chamber took place on December 19, 1962, in accordance with House Resolution 740, 87th Congress, 2nd Session. For this and the other Capitol Building mottoes, see House Document Number 362, 88th Congress, 2nd Session, *Compilation of Works of Art and Other Objects in the United States Capitol* (1965), p. 339.

I have adapted the interesting orientation diagram from a loose sheet from a French Masonic pamphlet dated 1790.

The Pyramid

65–66. The pyramid on the fifty-dollar bill, designed by Hopkinson in 1778, shows a doorway in the bottom row of pyramids. Such an entrance (though not on the first level of the pyramid) is found on the *north* face of the Great Pyramid at Giza. This might wrongly imply that the face of the pyramids on the Seal and dollar bill are intended to represent the north face. However, the drawing made by Hopkinson in 1778 was *not* of the Great Pyramid (his drawing is steeply stepped, out of all proportion to the prototype). When William Barton *did* use a stepped pyramid, based on the Great Pyramid, for his Seal proposal of 1782 (see drawing on page 94), he omitted the doorway.

Hopkinson's Masonic affiliation has been questioned— however, his father was a high-ranking Mason, and it seems unlikely that Hopkinson was not initiated. Many of the old records have been lost. The roundel depicting Barton's version of the reverse of the Seal is from a small detail at the top right of his second visualization for the Seal (see page 95).

67. Barton copied his pyramid (one presumes he traced it) from the foldout engraving in John Greaves's *Pyramidographia: or a Description of the Pyramids in Aegypt* (1646). The engraving of the pyramid, from which Barton traced his own proportions, had only eighty-nine steps—less than half the actual number. To make the truncation more noticeable, Barton sliced off the top two courses in the Greaves engraving. It is generally assumed that Barton copied his pyramid from the Hopkinson pyramid, in the engraving of the 1778 fifty-dollar bill. However, the Hopkinson pyramid is of a different proportion.

The only serious intimations that Hopkinson may have used the Greaves pyramid is the fact that the dark face is to the left of the pyramid—the opposite side of the dark face of the dollar pyramid, and the care with which Hopkinson drew in a door on the bottom course. This doorway certainly resembles the one the Greaves engraving, but (quite properly) Greaves showed the door within the fifth course of the north face.

For the quotation from Greaves regarding the "litle flat," see op. cit., p. 72. Greaves records the widely held opinion that the Egyptian priests had made their observations in astronomy from this platform. It is a belief that he himself refuted. Furthermore, the indications are that the Great Pyramid had been completed with the magical *ben-ben* stone, and therefore did come to a point.

John Greaves, English mathematician, linguist, and anti-quary, was born in Hampshire, England, in 1602; and after attending Balliol College, Oxford, he became professor of geometry at Gresham College. Starting in 1637, he began to travel widely in the Middle East, inspecting ancient sites, and collecting manuscripts in Arabic, Persian, and Greek. During this time, he visited Cairo on several occasions and made the first serious mathematical analysis of the Great Pyramid. On returning to England—where he wrote his important book on the pyramids in 1646 (see figure on page 96), he was made Savilian professor of astronomy at Oxford. He was deprived of this professorship because of his adherence to Charles I during the Civil War in England. He died in 1652.

For the precise measurements of the 202 remaining complete courses, see Piazzi Smyth, *Our Inheritance in the Great Pyramid*, (1880 enlarged edn.), pp. 94–95. The reference to the eleven camels is from the same source (p. 21).

68. A description of the truncated pyramid on the coat of arms of Pope Adrian VI is given in Bury Palliser, *Historic Devices, Badges and War-Cries* (1870), p. 222.

The engraving of *Art and Nature* is by the Dutch artist Reinier Boitet. It forms the frontispiece to *Het Groot Natuuren Zedekundigh Werelt Toneel of Woordenboek* (1743).

For an example of the pyramids on a Masonic apron, and for the Martin Folkes medal of 1724 and its relevance to the Egyptian mythology of Isis, see David Ovason, *The Secret Architecture of Our Nation's Capital* (2000), pp. 230–234.

69. The "triangled Pyramide" in the figure on page 99 is from George Wither, A *Collection of Emblems*, (1635), book 4, emblem X.

70. Manly Palmer Hall introduced the erroneous notion of the number of stones in the pyramid in his work, *The Secret Teachings of All Ages: An Encylopedic Outline of Masonic, Hermetic, Quabbalistic and Rosicrucian Symbolical Philosophy* (1928), p. xc. Manly Palmer Hall, born in Canada in 1901, founded the Los Angeles Philosophical Research Society in 1934. He was a Mason.

The diagram illustrating the seventy-two names of God is from Athanasius Kircher, *Oedipus Aegyptiacus* (1652–1654), vol. II, i, p. 287. The names in the outer concentric display Kircher's immense learning, for he gives the seventy-two names in as many languages. These languages are named alongside, in the contiguous concentric. A less complex listing of the seventy-two names is given, merely in Latin and Hebrew, by Julius Bartoloccius in *Bibliotheca Magna Rabbinica* (1675), vol. I, pp. 228–229.

For the 72 numerology of precession, see F. Gettings, *The Arkana Dictionary of Astrology* (1985 edn.), pp. 397–400.

71. The *tetractys* reproduced on page 103 is from Cornelius Agrippa, *De Occulta Philosophia*, book II, p. cxxvii. The most complex analysis of the Pythagorean *tetractys* is that offered by the Italian humanist Francesco Giorgio, whose *De Harmonia Mundi* (1525), influenced the thought of the English Rosicrucian, Robert Fludd.

Fludd's own *tetractys* was in ratio to the Great Pyramid, and visualized a descent from light into darkness (at the base of the pyramid): see *Philosophia sacra et vere Christiana seu Meteorologia Cosmica* (1626), p. 33. This contrast of light and darkness is that expressed in the Seal, and emphasized in the dollar-bill roundel.

72. The Tiffany color sketches of 1883 are preserved in the National Archives, Washington, D.C. (Record Group 59, entry 855). The radiant aura around the triangle seems to be unique in Seal design, and represents a brave attempt to introduce into the Seal a further example of the numerology of 13. The two sketches are reproduced by Patterson and Dougall, *The Eagle and the Shield* (1976 edn.), plate 39, p. 241.

At least five preliminary drawings were submitted by Tiffany & Company to the Department of State. Of these, only one of the reverses appears to have survived. Most of the Tiffany files relating to this matter were destroyed some time ago.

The report in the *Daily Graphic* appeared on May 14, 1885, p. 591.

For the Tiffany & Company report to Theodore F. Dwight, chief of the Bureau of Rolls and Library of the State Department, see Robert Hieronimus, *America's Secret Destiny* (1989 edn.), p. 85.

73. The suggestion that a Centennial Medal be minted was made by Charles A. L. Totten, then a first lieutenant stationed

at Sacketts Harbor, New York. Astonished that the symbolism on the reverse had been "allowed to remain so long in a state of neglect and concealment," he was inspired by the idea that the pyramid should be used in a commemorative medal. He entered into correspondence with Charles J. Folger, the Secretary of the Treasury, who agreed that such a medal should be minted. Folger passed Charles Totten on to A. Loudon Snowdon, the Superintendent of the Mint in Philadelphia, and a medal was eventually minted. After this experience, Totten wrote several works relating to the symbolism of the Seal, the most outstanding of which is *The Seal of History*, esp. vol. I, *Our Inheritance in the Great Seal of "Manasseh," the United States of America* (1897), which includes an account of the designing and minting of the commemorative medal.

The engraving, now called the Trenchard realization (because it was a graphic *realization*, or visualization, of the blazon for the reverse of the Seal), was engraved by James Trenchard of Philadelphia. It appeared as a frontispiece in the September 1786 issue of the *Columbian Magazine*. An original engraving is in the Library of the American Philosophical Society.

74. William McKinley was made a Mason in May 1865, in the Hiram No. 21 Lodge, Winchester, Virginia. One reason why he was in Chicago in that month is that he was to participate in the Masonic laying of the cornerstone of the Federal Post Office building. The McKinley speech of October 9, 1899, is recorded, in *Speeches and Addresses of William McKinley: From March 1, 1897, to May 30, 1900* (1900), pp. 243–247. The quoted passage is from pp. 245–47.

Magic Numbers

75–78. The Americans were, of course, forced into the date 1776. However, the designers of the Seal made much use of this in terms of a meaningful nine-figure chronogram.

There has been a long tradition of encoding meanings in numbers, chronograms, and dates, in what is called, in the magical tradition, the art of "Sacred Numbers." An excellent recent study of this tradition, as it was put to use in the seventeenth century, may be found in Ann Geneva, *Astrology and the Seventeenth-Century Mind* (1995), esp. chap. 2, "Aenigmaes, Metaphors, Parabols, and Figures": Seventeenth Century Encrypting." There were certain dangers in such encryptings. When Galileo announced, in a complex anagram, his discovery that the planet Saturn had rings, Kepler wrongly unscrambled the anagram to read an announcement that Saturn had two satellites. This was a belief continued into Swift's *Gulliver's Travels* (1726). See Geneva, op. cit., p. 33.

The designers of the Seal and dollar bill have played with several sacred numbers, the dominate one being 13. However, the 3 and 7, along with the product 21, is an important numerology. Behind many of the magical numbers lies the numerological reduction to 1—a reduction that is perfectly understandable in the light of the fact that this is a *one*-dollar bill. There is a magic in sounds: the numerical value of the sound dollar (D = 4, L = 30, A = 1, R = 200) is 235, which reduces to 10, which reduces to 1. Below, in 79, I offer a few interesting examples of the encoding of 33, which was one of the more important sacred numbers of the Rosicrucians.

For an account of Masonic number symbolism, see *The Freemason's Quarterly Review* (winter 1834), pp. 252ff.

79. Undoubtedly, the most sacred of all numbers is 33. It is therefore not surprising that it should have found its way into the encoding of the dollar bill. In particular, the 33 was used as an identification code in the Rosicrucian and alchemical traditions. It was a number adopted by Francis Bacon and used extensively by William Shakespeare. For example, Shakespeare, in *The First Part of King Henry the Fourth*, used the word *Francis* thirty-three times in a single column of text. For an examination of the code, see Frank Woodward, *Francis Bacon's Cipher Signatures* (1923). In the alchemical tradition, it was a favorite encoding designed to reveal, secretly, membership of the Rosicrucian fraternity. Almost certainly, the number was adopted because of its links with the life of Christ, who remained incarnate on earth for this period of years.

80. Hopkinson's first designs for his own proposal for the Seal (submitted by way of the Second Committee of 1780) are in the National Archives (*Papers of the Continental Congress*, item 23, folios 127,125, 133, and 135, Record Group 360).

81. The olive branch has been subjected to more numerical mutation than any other symbol on the dollar bill. The importance of the olive as a symbol of peace may be seen in the emblem book, by Henry Peacham, *Minerva Britanna* (1612), p. 145, in which image the crossed branches of olives have been placed below a radiant star of sixteen rays. Each olive branch has twenty-five leaves; there are eleven olives on the branches.

For Totten's observations, which led to the modern adoption of the thirteen leaves and thirteen olives, see Totten, *The Seal of History* (1897), Vol. 1, pp. 149–67.

The two Washington coins are from Crosby, *The Early Coins of America, and the Laws Governing Their Issue* (1875), p. 355.

82–85. Of the recurrence of the number 13 in the dollar bill (as we shall see, 13 is repeated thirteen times on the reverse!), little need be said: without doubt, the 13 is reference to the number of colonies that resisted Britain in those heady days towards the end of the eighteenth century. In fact, the number 13 may be described as the mainspring numerology of American art.

The Eagle

86. For the symbolism of the eagle, see, Rudolf Wittkower, *Allegory and the Migration of Symbols* (1977), pp. 16ff. The woodcut of the Great Comet of 1577 is from Marcellus Squarcialupus, *De cometis dissertationes novae* (1580). For the Eagle as the Living Eye, see R. H. Allen, *Star Names: Their Lore and Meaning* (1963 edn.), p. 56. The Metropolitan Museum Christ-and-eagle is on the *Antioch Chalice*.

87. For Honnecourt's pentagrammic eagle, see J. B. A. Lassus, *Album de Villard de Honnecourt: Architecte du xiiie siècle. Manuscrit publié en facsimile annoté* (1858), plate xxxv.

For possible interpretations of Rudolph's ADSIT motto, see Bury Palliser, *Historic Devices, Badges and War Cries* (1870), p. 89.

88. William Barton's proposal that the eagle should represent Congress is found in his explanation of the symbols, consequent to the written blazon. The eagle signifies Congress because it is a symbol of supreme power and authority. See *The Papers of the Continental Congress*, item 23, folios 137–139. In his second proposal, he indicated that the eagle was expressive of sovereignty. See *The Papers of the Continental Congress*, item 23, folios 139–142. These papers have been printed in full in Patterson and Dougall, *The Eagle and the Shield* (1976) pp. 60–63.

89. For Colonna and the eagle as symbol of Jupiter and Imperial Majesty, see Guy de Tervarent, *Attributs et Symboles dans l'Art Profane 1450–1600: Dictionnaire d'un Langage Perdue* (1958), pp. 5–6. For the eagle as representative of the sense of sight, see ibid. p. 6. Tervarent gives several examples in art, and quotes Isidore of Seville, *Etymologiarum libri XX* (lib. XII, chap. 7) as a source. So important was the association, in late medieval times, between the eagle and sight that the etymologists claimed, in their quaint way, that the Latin word for the bird (*aquila*) was derived from *acumine* ("acuteness"). The bestiaries, which recount this fiction, seem to associate the eagle with the phoenix, for they grant it the power of renewal—not from flames, but from water. See, for example, T. H. White, *The Book of Beasts: Being a Translation from a Latin Bestiary of the Twelfth Century* (1956 edn.), pp. 105–8. The drawing of the solarized eagle in this section is copied from a medieval manuscript drawing, reproduced by White.

90. The alchemical engraving, depicting the four sigils for the elements, is from Johann Daniel Mylius, *Philosophia Reformata*, (1622), engraving no. 2.

91. For the original design for the dollar bill, signed and approved by Roosevelt, see 8.

92. William Barton's drawing for his first proposal has been lost. His second, which is a watercolor drawing and which forms the basis for the drawing on page 135 in this section, is in the National Archives, Washington, D.C. Because of its fragility, it is not on public display: it is in the *Papers of the Continental Congress*, item, 23, folio 117, Record Group 360.

93. Manly Palmer Hall had borrowed the phoenix print from the first edition of Sir J. Gardner Wilkinson's book, *The Manners and Customs of the Ancient Egyptians* (1837). However, in the later edition of this work, Wilkinson admitted

that he had made a mistake about the identity of this image. Wilkinson's note, to the effect that the bird-man did not represent the phoenix, appears in vol. III, p. 328 of the 1878 edition of the book. Manly Hall continued to publish the drawing as a representative of the phoenix in his later editions of the work. I have consulted the ninth edition of this work, published in 1947, wherein the material is represented on page XC. The heraldic eagle is copied from Henry Goodyere, *The Mirrour of Maiestie* (1618), emblem 4.

94. For William Barton's phoenix, see 92.

95. The work on heraldry owned by Benjamin Franklin was Joachim Camerarius, *Symbolorum ac emblematum ethico-politicorum centuriae quatuor* (1702). The drawing on page 139 is based on an engraving in this work. This work is now in the Library Company of Philadelphia—see *Annual Report* (1956), pp. 7–19.

The roundel depicting the alchemical eagle is a detail from Johann Daniel Mylius, *Anatomiae Auri sive tyrocinium medicochymicum* (1628); it is one of the twelve images designed to illustrate the Philosopher's Stone—from Part V, p. 26.

96. Jefferson's "bundle of rods" idea may be traced to a period after the meeting of the first committee, of which Jefferson was a member. See Julian P. Boyd, *The Papers of Thomas Jefferson* (1950), I, p. 495. The bear emblem is from George Wither, *A Collection of Emblems* (1635), book p. 3, emb. xliii.

Some Deeper Mysteries Behind the Dollar Bill

97. The New Testament references to Christ as the stone are in, Matthew 21:42–44; Mark 12:10; Luke 20:17–18, Acts 4:11; 1 Peter 2:4-8; the communal source reference seems to be

Psalm 118:22 in the Old Testament, with a subreference to Isaiah, 28:16.

For the new approach to the meaning of the stone, see A. K. Coomaraswamy, "Eckstein," in *Speculum* XIV (1939), pp. 66ff. See also, Gerhart B. Ladner, "The Symbolism of the Biblical Corner Stone in the Mediaeval West," in *Images and Ideas in the Middle Ages: Selected Studies in History and Art* (1983), pp. 171ff. The Latin *caput anguli* is, in Greek, *eis kephalen gonias*, and, in Hebrew, *lerosch pinna*. This corresponds to the Egyptian *ben-ben*, which is the name given to the final triangular stone, with which the pyramid is capped.

For the reference to Saint Augustine of Hippo, see his *Enarrationes in Psalm.* LXXXVI 1 f., pl. 37, 1101ff., quoted in Latin in Ladner, pp. 180–81. For example, in Matthew 21:42, the reference in Latin is to the *caput anguli*, which must be translated as "the head of the angle." This Latin corresponds to the words in both Greek and Aramaic.

98. For the relationship between the star Sothis and the pyramid, see W. Marsham Adams, *The Book of the Master of the Hidden Places* (1933), pp. 28–33. The significance of the *ben-ben* stone has been discussed by Robert Bauval and Adrian Gilbert, *The Orion Mystery* (1994): these two authors emphasize the connection between the *ben-ben* and the *bennu*, or phoenix.

There is an excellent color reproduction of the Amenemhat III *ben-ben* in W. Forman and S. Quirke, *Hieroglyphics and the Afterlife in Ancient Egypt* (1996), p. 73. This is carved in black basalt and must have contrasted strongly with the white facing of the pyramid itself. This contrast is reflected in the drawing we examined on page 146.

For Sothis/Sirius, see Allen, *Star Names: Their Lore and Meaning* (1963), pp. 120–29.

For Sirius as the original blazing star of the Masons, see David Ovason, *The Secret Architecture of Our Nation's Capital: The Masons and the Building of Washington, D.C.* (2000), for example, pp. 4–5, 117–18.

The lines of Alfred, Lord Tennyson, quoted towards the end of this section, are from his *The Princess: A Medley* (first edn., 1857), p. 107. The variations in color between red and emerald may verge on poetic license, but the star *is* a binary, and it does appear to scintillate more insistently than other stars.

99. Totten's remarkable idealization of the reverse of the Seal is from *The Seal of History. Volume 11. Our Inheritance in The Great Seal of "Manasseh," The United States of America* (1897), p. 265.

100. The engraving of the Diplomatic Medal given by Totten, *The Seal of History* (1897), vol. 1, p. 153, does not do justice to the radiation of the glory. Totten's engraving shows the radiants emerging from below the left wing of the eagle, whereas in the original medal the radiants emerge also below the right wing. The reverse of the Diplomatic Medal of 1792 is reproduced by Patterson and Dougall, *The Eagle and the Shield* (1976), p. 393, plate 65.

BOOKS BY DAVID OVASON

THE SECRET ARCHITECTURE
OF OUR NATION'S CAPITAL
*The Masons and the Building
of Washington, D.C.*
ISBN 0-06-095368-3 (trade paperback)
Ovason's richly illustrated text tells the story of how
Washington, D.C., from its foundation in 1791, was
linked to the zodiac, with the meaning of certain stars,
and how even the art, architecture, and city geography
embody hidden cosmological symbolism.

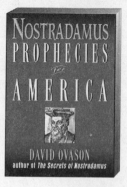

NOSTRADAMUS
Prophecies for America
ISBN 0-06-009351-X (mass market paperback)
On September 11, catastrophe struck America. Five
hundred years ago, Nostradamus predicted it would occur.
In this book, internationally renowned Nostradamus
expert David Ovason examines Nostradamus'
work regarding American history
and his predictions for our future.

THE SECRETS OF NOSTRADAMUS
*A Radical New Interpretation
of the Master's Prophecies*
ISBN 0-06-008439-1 (trade paperback)
David Ovason cracks the Green Language
code in this book that contains
the most accurate translation of
Nostradamus' true predictions.

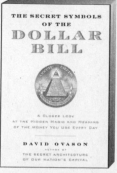

THE SECRET SYMBOLS OF THE DOLLAR BILL
*A Closer Look at the Hidden Magic and
Meaning of the Money You Use Every Day*
ISBN 0-06-053045-6 (trade paperback)
The fascinating and long-buried secret meanings behind
the symbols on the dollar bill and the reason the Founding
Fathers crafted it in such a way.